How to Publish an Indie Book

AN ASYMMETRICAL GUIDE

Asymmetrical Press
Missoula, Montana

Published by Asymmetrical Press, Missoula, Montana.

Library of Congress Cataloging-In-Publication Data
How to Write and Publish and Indie Book / Asymmetrical Press — 1st ed.
ISBN: 978-1-938793-89-9
eISBN: 978-1-938793-90-5
WC: 24,705
1. Publishing. 2. Writing. 3. How-to. 4. Independent authors. 5. Indie publishing.

Cover design by Colin Wright
Formatted in beautiful Montana
Printed in the U.S.A.

Publisher info:
Website: www.asymmetrical.co
Email: howdy@asymmetrical.co
Twitter: @asympress

ASYM METR ICAL

For the indie at heart.

"Writing is a form of personal freedom. It frees us from the mass identity we see in the making all around us. In the end, writers will write not to be outlaw heroes of some underculture but mainly to save themselves, to survive as individuals."

—Don DeLillo

CONTENTS

How to Publish
an Indie Book

FOREWARD: THANK YOU

We started Asymmetrical with a few guiding principles in mind.

The first was that we wanted to build a company that kept authors in control. They take the majority of the profits from their work, they have final cut on editing, covers, and anything else that has their name on it, and they are also in control of (and responsible for) the growth of their audience, platforms, and brand.

The second was that we wanted to be able to experiment within the publishing space and see what we could push or bend, and what we could change completely. We've been able to dabble in this area so far—especially in ensuring our authors are able to be multidisciplinarians with their craft, while still improving their mastery over a core focus—and have engaged in a multitude of small experiments thus far, with slightly larger ones just over the horizon.

And finally, we wanted to build a company that would sustain itself as a business, but also allow us to invest in the publishing community as a whole. This was a tricky principle to fulfill, but we've built a decent-sized (and thriving) Community of publishers and authors, which has proven to be a hot-bed for ideas and inspiration as to what we should do next.

More than anything else, we've had people asking for a cohesive overview of how to publish a book. They might understand how to write, but not how to produce an ebook file from their work. Or maybe they have the file, but don't have a cover. Or know how to convert their ebook to a print book. Or know how to build an audience. Or understand how they get paid.

It's a complicated world, publishing, and especially difficult for authors and would-be authors who don't have the time to spend doing an immense amount of research and engage in the (sometimes troubling) amount of trial-and-error required to really understand the subtleties of the process.

To that end, we decided to write down everything we could think of that might be worth knowing. We wanted to share our entire process, and to make it as accessible, actionable, and comprehensive as possible. We shared it as a blog series, each (sometimes massive) post focusing on a different step in the indie publishing process. And with each post we recorded an accompanying podcast episode of 20-30 minutes where we expand upon that part of the process, sharing our personal experiences with it, and other tidbits that it might help to understand beyond the write-up.

We wrote that blog series over a year ago, and since then we've wanted to take that blog series, take what we learned about publishing an indie book, and share it, aptly, as a book. This is that book. Thank you for purchasing it—by doing so, you've helped support a community of independent creators and artists, and you've also helped support indie publishing as a whole.

We appreciate you.

The Asymmetrical Team
2015

A PREAMBLE-ISH OPENING STATEMENT: WHAT IS INDIE PUBLISHING?

Damn we hate introductions. Like, a lot. Most intros are vapid and ephemeral and can usually be ignored. The word *prolegomenous* comes to mind. But this here little lead-in seems, if not apropos, at least somewhat necessary considering the weight of what we hope to communicate with this book: viz., we want to present to you a detailed, step-by-step, how-to guide for publishing an Indie Book that is indistinguishable in every way—quality, content, editing, book cover, formatting, printing, distribution, promotion—from Books published by the industry's Big Six Publishers. Nevertheless, feel free to dismiss this opening section, to move on to the meatier parts that follow.

Still here? Oh, well, so then here's an introduction of sorts…

Over the course of six short-ish chapters, we'll show you, based on our own experience as successful Independent Authors, how to publish an Indie Book (hence the title).

This book includes six chapters:

1. How to Write a Book
2. How to Edit and Proofread Your Book
3. How to Create a Book Cover, Author Bio, and Synopsis for Your Book
4. How to Format Your Book for Print, Ebook, and Audiobook
5. How to Distribute Your Book via Various Sales Channel
6. How to Successfully Promote Your Book to an Audience

We welcome your feedback and questions on all the information you find here. Feel free to tweet at us: @AsymPress.

Bear with us. This whole thing is a little strange to us because we don't typically write "how-to" books; instead we tend to address the "why-to," which is, for the most part, far more important (i.e., without the *why*, the *how* is fairly trivial). However, we believe that the "how-to" in this case is direly important; it's a big hurdle for many would-be-published Authors, and so we want to help.

Thus, two things'll likely occur throughout these six

chapters. First, you'll probably find handfuls of "why-to" (purpose-driven) ruminations peppered throughout the entire book (especially within the first chapter). This seems unavoidable; we like to ruminate. Second, we won't show you *the* path to publishing your Book; we'll uncover *a* path —our path—which you're welcome to follow. Basically, we'll show you our recipe, including which ingredients have and haven't worked for us, and then you're welcome (even encouraged) to add your own ingredients to suit your taste.

End banal intro. Fade into meaty parts.

Adding Value

We started Asymmetrical for a laundry list of reasons, but all those reasons point back to one underlying goal: Adding Value. If Asymmetrical has a single objective, that's it. We know that if we add enough value to enough people through Asymmetrical, then we'll be able to raise the tide of Independent Publishing, not just our own work, but Indie Publishing as a whole. That way everyone benefits; a rising tide lifts all boats.

Adding Value is the reason we started the Asym Community, in which we encourage Authors and other creative types to exchange value with each other, sharing tips and best practices and resources just like, well, a *community*—a community that grows together.

Adding Value is the reason we work with a small group of Authors from our Community, experimenting with their work so we can share our discoveries with the world. These Authors don't allow us to function as a Traditional Publisher (that was never our intent). Rather, our Authors are the (cute, cuddly, fuzzy) lab rats from whom we learn more about the Independent Publishing Process, learnings that we're able to pass on to you via the Community, the Asym Blog, and books like this one.

Adding Value is also the reason we work with more than 40 outstanding interns—our talented Asymmetrical People—who are themselves working hard to help us help you.

And Adding Value should be every Author's objective when writing a Book, as well.

In fact, Adding Value is the reason we've put together this Guide. We want to prove to you that you needn't worship at the altar of the old guard, that you needn't "submit" to anyone. You can successfully publish on your own, soup to nuts, controlling every morsel of the Process.

The present day is the most exciting time in history to be an Author. No longer are you beholden to the gatekeepers; no longer must you compromise your art. For the first time in publishing history, you are in control. We know this first hand. The Authors of this Guide aren't some hacks who just write about writing. Nope. Rather, when we weren't happy with the publishing landscape, we took matters into our own hands; we refused to wait for someone else's permission to publish our work.

And guess what: we've been successful. We've published over 30 Books (nonfiction, fiction, and memoirs), several of which have been bestsellers; we've toured internationally; and we've established audiences larger than most Traditionally Published Authors.

But that's because we're not just Authors, and neither are you.

Authors as Businesspeople

You see, there was a time when an Author was just an author. At that time, their focus was on writing the best Book they could possibly write. Someone else would edit, lay out, design, market, sell, and publish the Book, which was a deal that most Authors were fine with, at least partially because it was the only option available.

The big downside to that arrangement is that someone else also owned their work. Authors would sell the rights to their Book to a publisher, and that publishing company would pay them a small advance (i.e., a loan) and then a small percentage of revenue generated by sales (after the advance was paid back).

It was a decent living for the fortunate few who made it past the several rounds of gatekeepers between them and bookstore shelves, and for some it's still a good option.

Today there are other options, though, and we feel strongly that even Authors in Traditional Publishing arrangements should see their writing as assets and treat them as such. They should be in control of their own promotional efforts and social media content. They should be aware of what is worth what, and which methods of delivery are available on a given project.

Of course, for Authors who are independently publishing their work, this goes double. In order to really succeed—apart from the outside chance of being "discovered" and showered with money—it's best to view yourself as an entrepreneur, not just an Author. An *Authorpreneur*. A creative businessperson.

This perspective allows a creative person to look at each business challenge as an opportunity to enhance their work and get it out to more people. Businessy tasks—like updating social media and converting published work into multiple formats—become one more part of the Creative Process, which they are, if you're doing them right.

The business of publishing, as well as the published work itself, must be high quality if the reading public is going to be exposed and open to investing their time and money in Indie Work. If you're doing it right, the experience of purchasing and consuming your work should be as good as the work itself.

What Exactly Is "Indie" Publishing?

For the longest time, Indie Publishing had a bad reputation.

It was most often associated with so-called Vanity Publishing, which essentially meant that you wrote a Book and then paid to have it published yourself. The derogatory nature of the moniker stemmed from the idea that if a Book hadn't gone through the gauntlet of Traditional Publishing, it probably wasn't worth very much.

And in most cases, the Books did *seem* quite sub-par, even if they were well-written. The paper quality was off. The design was laughable. Details we've come to expect from published work—like ISBN numbers, copyright pages, and bastard title pages—weren't evident, and their lack made us question what the Author was trying to achieve by converting their hard-earned money into pseudo-published work.

Independent Publishing today is quite a different creature.

Today there are small presses operating on models similar to those of larger publishing companies (though generally with more favorable contracts for the Authors) putting out work that rivals or beats that of the Big Six.

There are Independent Authors doing the same, and with the same level of quality and success. In the last year, even Authors who make advances in the hundreds of thousands or millions of dollars have been leaving their publishers to operate solo. They learn the ropes of the industry themselves, or (more commonly) hire Independent Editors, Designers, Marketers, Publicists, Website Designers, and anyone else they need to make their Book a success on bookshelves.

In short, we live in a time where Traditional Publishing finally has a legitimate rival, and that rival is each and every Author with a computer and WiFi signal.

We don't say this to hate on Traditional Publishing—they have long done good work, and still do—but we're giddily excited about the potential that things like eBooks, on-demand publishing, and the interconnectivity of social media have brought to the forefront. This is a time of great uncertainty, but uncertain times are when new normals are born.

Also birthed from uncertain times are great Books. And writing a Book is the important first step in the long Publishing Process. So let's chat about writing one, shall we?

CHAPTER 1: HOW TO WRITE A BOOK

So, you're writing a Book, eh? Or maybe you've already written one and it's collecting dust or rejection letters or both. Or maybe you just know deep down that you have a Book inside you that's waiting to pour itself onto the blank page.

The Hardest Part

Well, dearest Author, we have good/bad news for you: writing a Book is by far the most difficult step in the Publishing Process. Hence, that's great news if you've already written a Book you're happy with (if that's the case you might want to move on to Chapter 2), but it's bad news if you've yet to start.

Moreover, writing a Book is one thing. Writing an

interesting Book that adds value to people's lives is thorny and intricate and considerably more complicated. But don't fret, Author; we brought a proverbial flashlight to help illuminate the way (does anyone have an extra set of C batteries?).

First, we should start with a relevant question: What the Hell Is a Book?

What the Hell Is a Book?
(An Essay by Joshua Fields Millburn)

What is a book? Seriously, it's a valid question, so please bracket your skepticism for a moment, and let's think about it together.

During the first day of my writing class,[1] I query my students: What is a book? I ask them to think about it for the next few weeks, and then we discuss the concept during our final class, four weeks later.

You see, "What is a book?" used to be a question with a relatively easy answer: a printed work consisting of pages glued or sewn together along one side and bound in covers. Traditionally, books of standard size were roughly 70,000 words, usually 200–300 pages.

But traditional books were a standard size because their publishers needed to charge a standard price. That is, roughly $25 allowed publishers to pay for marketing, advertising, printing, editing, formatting, distribution, shelving, executive bonuses, etc. And sometimes, after all the expenses were paid, they recouped enough money to pay a book's author a few shillings. Sometimes.

These days, though, a book has the potential to be much different. We as writers and readers are no longer relegated by the requirements of old. No longer does a book *need* to be 70,000 words. Thus, many contemporary books are short—drastically shorter in some cases. My friend, *New York Times* bestselling author Julien Smith, wrote a short book called *The Flinch*,[2] which is only about 10,000 words. *The Flinch* could have been much longer—in fact was much longer during its first draft—but Julien attenuated it by focusing on only the essential content, rewriting the final draft "one tweet at a time." The result is a much more powerful book, a book that removed the fat, a book in which every page is spilling quotable lines (e.g., "The strength you gain by letting go is more important than any object you own.")

Similarly, Shawn Mihalik's beautiful novella, *The Flute Player*,[3] is just 105 pages, and most of my books are condensed compared to books of old, averaging less than 30,000 words in most cases (my novel being the exception, but even it was radically attenuated from 950 pages to fewer than 300). I've learned that in a world of Twitter and Facebook and iEverything, our attention spans have become condensed, and thus we must work harder to produce meaningful work that is also condensed. That doesn't mean that there isn't room for 1,000-page books like *Infinite Jest* or *The Instructions*; it just means that we have more options, and that length can now be dictated by the content, not the need to fill a certain number of pages. If a book needs to be 1,000+ pages, that's great. If it needs to be 40 pages, that's great too.

Because book length is changing, the vehicles in which books are delivered are also different. Thus, our reading options are more diverse than ever before, and they are becoming more and more diverse every day. Accordingly, to serve the sundry needs of my readership, I make my books available in multiple formats: paperback, ebook via Kindle, and even audiobook via Audible and iTunes. Other people make their books available in other non-traditional formats as well: iBooks, Nook, Smashwords, PDF, blog posts, and even social media (e.g., Rick Moody's "Some Contemporary Characters"[4] is a wonderfully alive story that was published on Twitter, one tweet at a time).

As vehicles change, so does the price of books. *The Flinch* is free as a Kindle book. And most of my books are $5 or less on Kindle (a couple of them are just a buck), while their printed versions are priced higher to cover the printing costs. But none of my books are even close to $25, because I don't have all the bloat of the middlemen syphoning the revenue into their pockets. Because my books are cheaper, I can reach more people, and because I believe in my books, I know that people who find value in them will recommend them to friends. Such referrals are my one true marketing strategy: that is, add value and people will share.

This is why I've had several bestsellers, not marketing hype or advertising.

Amid all the change, bookstores are changing, too. We've all noticed the big chains going by the wayside over the past few years. If you're anything like me, you were upset to see this change. Personally, I love bookstores—I love the smell, the look, the feel of books—and so do many other people. Ergo, I don't think bookstores are going away anytime soon. But, like everything else, the bookstore experience is going to encounter radical changes in the years to come. Some bookstores will become more niche, more specialized, more boutique-y, while others will focus more on the customer experience, creating the atmosphere that gets readers in their doors. Almost all bookstores will become decentralized in the future, more local, which will appeal to folks in the community much more than the mega-stores (think farmer's market vs. Walmart's produce section).

Times are a-changin'. For that reason, there's never been a more exciting time to be a writer. If you embrace the change, you will flourish. If you don't, you can set up a tent in a Borders parking lot and wait for things to go back to the way they were. Good luck.

As you can see, a Book isn't even easy to *define* anymore, let alone write. But we'd like to posit to you that a Book's undefinability is a good thing; it gives you, the Writer, more flexibility, which might make it a bit easier to finish.

Deadlines

There are at least two types of Authors: the kind who flourish under pressure and the kind whose nervous system is so weak that even the thought of potential pressure nearly incapacitates them. That is to say, there are Writers who need deadlines/goals/objectives and Writers who do not.

The former are propelled forward by deadlines. Seriously, we've witnessed Colin Wright write a draft of an entire Book, cover to cover, in a day. We shit you not. (In contrast, it takes some of us several days just to write a single blog post.) These Writers often produce their best work when they're under the gun.

The latter, however, will, at best, wince at the mere mention of a deadline; or at worst, they'll get nauseated and need to find something soft to sit on. These Writers are more creative when the Process is drawn out, boundless, abstract. Their writing often appears concise and deliberate in its final iteration, even gorgeous at times, but there's usually buckets of words left on the cutting room floor during the Editing Process (N.B. we'll discuss the Editing Process in detail in Chapter 2). In short, give them a deadline, and you most certainly won't get their best work.

Suffice it to say, you yourself must (to use an overused idiom) take a long look in the mirror and figure out which kind of Writer you are. Be honest—it's for *your* benefit. If you're not sure, or you're somewhere in the middle, then set-up some Draconian rules by which to gauge your Process. Give yourself strict deadlines. If they help, great! Keep them.

What we've discovered is that 98 out of 100 times, deadlines help Authors write the Book they want to write, especially for newer Writers who don't already write several hours a day.

A Writer's Support System

Equally as important as deadlines is a Writer's support system, especially when it comes to finishing your Book. Actually, your Support System and your deadline often work in conjunction to hurl your Book over its finish line.

Support from peers, family, friends, etc. is paramount, so much so in fact that Joshua requires every student in his writing class to acquire an Accountability Partner on the first day. He does this because he knows how much it helped him when he first started writing. His Accountability Partner kept him, *ahem*, accountable. Hence, each day his students must take 90 seconds to send a QAR, a Quick Accountability Report (which, by the way, is just a fancy term for *email*), to their AP. The QAR contains three simple lines:

- How much did I write today?
- What did I write about?
- How do I feel about the writing? Was it a good day or a bad day? Why?

Feel free to do likewise, as well as to modify the QAR to your specific needs/objectives. If you have trouble locating an AP among your friends and family, see if someone in our Community[5] is willing to help.

Your Support System extends way beyond your AP, though. Your Support System really contains anyone who is supportive of you and your work as a Writer. That means anyone, truly anyone: loved ones, co-workers, people who are close to you, acquaintances, and yes, even total strangers. Your SS helps fuel your excitement for writing.

Yes, we know you're passionate about writing your Book, but passion doesn't necessarily equal excitement. It's important, then, to find excitement via external stimulation (hey, get your mind out of the gutter). To do so, talk about your Book with everyone who's willing to listen. Tell them what it's about; tell them why you're writing it; express to them how passionate you are.

This sounds silly, we know. But the more you talk about it, the more excited you'll be, and thus the more you'll take action.

Together, your AP and the entirety of your SS

will catapult you from undone to done quicker than you think.

Prioritizing Your Time

The single biggest excuse we hear for why people don't write as much as they should—why they never finish their Book—is "I don't have enough time." How lame. Let's go take a peek at that metaphorical mirror again.

It's time for you to be honest with yourself. Either you're accomplishing what you want to accomplish or you're not. You're either writing that Book or you're not. There is no in-between. If it's the latter, then you must admit to yourself that *you* are the only person preventing you from pursuing your passion project. Denial is a heartless bitch; so, if it's true, then the first step is admitting that you haven't even scratched the surface.

As for the time excuse, none of us were born equal. We come from different backgrounds, different cultures, different socioeconomic situations. We were not all born on a level playing field. *Time* is the one exception. The only thing we all have in common is time. We all have the same 24 hours in a day. So, get up at 3:30 A.M.[6] if you have to. Find 30 minutes before you leave for work. Work through your lunch break. Find an hour after work. If you want it bad enough, you'll find the time. You have the same amount of time as everyone else who has ever written a Book.

It's time, then, to start killing your distractions, to finally make writing your Book a real priority, instead of it residing on your wish list.

Take a look at your day-to-day life. Through the hustle and bustle of your daily grind, what banal, tedious, mundane tasks eat up most of your time? Checking email? Monkeying around on Facebook? Watching television? Filling out reports?

Whatever your answer, these activities are your *true* priorities.

Yet we often claim that our priorities are grandly important activities like spending time with family or exercising or carving out enough alone time to work on that Book we've been putting off. But unless you're actually putting these pursuits first, unless you make these undertakings part of your everyday routine, they are not your actual priorities.

Your priorities are what you do each day, the small tasks that move forward the second and minute hands on the clock. These circadian endeavors are your *musts*. Everything else is simply a *should. I should do this. I should do that. I should, I should, I should.* Too often, we should all over ourselves. You must instead make change a *must. I must write my Book! I must make time every day! I must kill my distractions!* Those *musts* sound far more empowering than your *shoulds*, don't they?

To Outline or Not To Outline

There are two camps in the outline debate: 1) Yes, you should start with an outline, and 2) No, don't worry 'bout it.

We don't have a membership card to either camp. Ultimately, we think the Outlining Process is highly individual and is based more on personal preference than any set of guiding principles.

Some Writers always start *without* an outline, producing volumes and volumes of text that will be radically reduced later (Joshua Fields Millburn's 280-page novel, *As a Decade Fades,*[7] for example, was originally 950 pages before he attenuated it). Then, when the Book begins to take shape, often after a violent, almost incoherent first draft, they go back and outline the Book, looking for structural elements that work well together. The resulting outline ends up being invaluable during the Re-writing and Editorial Processes.

Other Writers, on the other hand, must always have an outline before they begin. They must produce a map of the journey before embarking on it.

And there are some Writers, still, who refuse the map altogether, opting instead to just drive in a direction and see where that takes them.

No one way is right or wrong; it simply depends on the person. Again, like deadlines, our best advice is to start with an outline, see if you need it, and then act accordingly.

Proofreading: Ask for Help

The Writing Process itself is highly personal for almost every Writer, so personal that sometimes it seems intrusive to even talk about it. But for your benefit, we will.

Writers often spend hours a day—two or three or four, sometimes ten or eleven or twelve—in a room, splashing words (handwritten and typed) onto blank pages. It's a lonely, but satisfying, exercise. What's worse is that we Writers spend so much time with our words, our thoughts, our stories, that we can't usually find the forest through the pines in our own work. After a while, our writing, no matter how good it might be, looks like a jumbled mess to our too-familiar eyes.

The solution is simple: find a clean pair of eyes.

We have a few alpha-readers who read our stuff before anyone else—less than a handful of people from whom, when we have something rough draftish we can share, we solicit honest feedback. We trust these folks' opinions immensely.

Proofreading can seem overwhelming, and typos are a yucky burden. So eradicating as many typos as possible from your manuscript before you go through the editing process is important. You can find folks on your own or via the Asym Community. And you can even take it a step farther and hire a professional Proofreader (who is different from an Editor, which we'll discuss in Chapter 2). That is, once you've incorporated your alpha-readers' feedback into your Manuscript, it's often wise to also find a Professional Proofreader to seek out and destroy as many errors as possible before you move on to the Editing Process.

Copyright Info

From the Library of Congress:

While copyright in the United States automatically attaches upon the creation of an original work of authorship, registration with the Copyright Office puts a copyright holder in a better position if litigation arises over the copyright. A copyright holder desiring to register his or her copyright should do the following:

1. *Obtain and complete appropriate form.*[8]
2. *Prepare clear rendition of material being submitted for copyright*
3. *Send both documents to U.S. Copyright Office in Washington, D.C.*

Registration of copyright refers to the act of registering the work with the United States Copyright Office, which is an office of the Library of Congress. As the United States has joined the Berne Convention, registration is no longer necessary to provide copyright protection. However, registration is still necessary to obtain statutory damages in case of infringement.

Copyright Act § 407 provides that the owner of copyright in a published or unpublished work may, at any time during the copyright, register the work with the Copyright Office. The purpose of the registration provisions is to create as comprehensive a record of U.S. copyright claims as is possible. To register, the registrant must complete an application form and send it, along with the filing fee and copies of the work, to the Copyright Office.

The Copyright Office reviews applications for obvious errors or lack of copyrightable subject matter, and then issues a certificate of registration.

Registration as a prerequisite to claim of moral rights violation: it's not necessary for any Author to register prior to bringing suit for violation of the rights of attribution or integrity in a work of visual art, pursuant to Copyright Act § 106A.

So basically, once you write something, it's already copyrighted. You can "officially" copyright it if you want, but it's not totally necessary unless you need to file a lawsuit.

Value of the Book: The Payoff

Ultimately, a Book is finished when it fulfills two criteria:

1. **Is your Book interesting?** Of course, no matter how

interesting it might be, not everyone is going interested in your Book, but if *you* were the Reader (not the Author, but the actual person who has to buy the Book and spend his or her time plowing through page after page), would you find it interesting, compelling, urgent? Is it fun and/or funny? Do you want to keep reading? Sometimes it helps to put the Book away for a month and then re-approach it as a Reader. Be honest and give yourself critical feedback.

2. **Is there a payoff?** This is the most important aspect of a finished Book. Will your Readers—who by the way have to put massive amounts of time and attention into reading your damn Book—will they receive a sufficient enough payoff for the time and money they've spent? Really—will they *really* receive a payoff? Is reading your Book the best use of their time? If so, why? What is the payoff? Countless Books are littered with bad writing, with little or no value, and thus no payoff. This sort of bad writing is usually written by timid, careless Writers who don't consider the Reader. We have one bit of advice for these Writers: cut the shit. Stop wasting people's precious time. Instead, work tirelessly to hone your skills, to craft a Book that is meaningful and urgent and interesting. Work your ass off to write a Book that matters, a Book with a payoff. It's worth it in the end.

Further listening: Podcast: How to Write a Book: (http:// asymmetrical.co/?powerpress_pinw=1314-podcast)

Further reading: Considering Your Readership (http://asymmetrical.co/readership/)

CHAPTER 2: HOW TO EDIT AND PROOFREAD YOUR BOOK

Times They Are a-Changing

Historically, one of biggest advantages Traditional Publishing had over Indie Publishing was the rigorous work that went into editing a Book. Published Authors had at their beck and call talented Editors, Line-Editors, Copyeditors, and even proofreading Interns. These folks— pros, the lot of them—were all integral parts of a Book's maturation toward print. *Were* being the key word here.

But today, as Caleb Pirtle points out, "[E]ditors have become an endangered species."[9]

It's not that the Big Six don't want the work to be good; they do. And it's not like they want to publish unedited Books; they don't. They simply want you, the

Author, to—ahem—Do It Yourself. That is, they expect their authors to self-edit, just like—ahem, ahem—Indie Authors. In other words, unless you're a Bestselling Author with a track record, don't expect a publisher to take your work, work it over, and polish it till it shines. It simply doesn't work that way anymore.

Here's the Deal, Kids

An Author without an Editor is a hot mess, coffee without a coffee cup.

The way Big Publishers used to publish Books, a Process fraught with overzealous Editors donning pocket protectors brimming with red pens, was actually a great way to produce great art. A good Editor not only improves a Writer's work, he improves a Writer's future work, too. In addition to regular copyediting—fishing for typos and grammatical/syntactical errors—an Editor helps his Author shape her voice, strengthening the Book *and* the Author.

A good Editor makes you feel like you've been beaten with a hammer, only to realize afterward you look better with bruises and fewer teeth. That's the role they play in your life—they help you carve away the excess, even when some of what needs to be removed is hair and skin and bone. At the end of the day, it will be worth it.

At Asymmetrical Press, we've independently published over 30 Books, and we've learned a ton about editing in the

Process, losing a lot of hair and several teeth with each Book. A few years ago, though, when each of us started publishing Books, we approached the Editing Process haphazardly, timidly. We didn't know much about editing. We didn't know the difference between proofreading and editing, between content editing and copyediting, between Final Draft and First Edition.

Over time, we learned from our mistakes. Each time we published a Book, it got better, tighter, stronger. Eventually an Editing Process formed, which we formalized for our Authors, as well as our own Books. We'd like to share it with you...

Asymmetrical's Editing Process

We developed a 10-step editorial checklist to guide us through the Editing Process for each Book we publish. It looks like this:

1. **Author Completes Manuscript**. This means write the Book. Go back to Chapter 1 if you missed this step.

2. **Author Sends Manuscript to 6–12 Alpha-Readers**. Once you've written your Book, you'll want half-a-dozen to a dozen clean pairs of eyes to look it over, provide honest feedback, and point out obvious mistakes. Solicit friends and colleagues you trust.

3. **Author Incorporates Alpha-Readers' Feedback**. Don't be so married to an idea that you're not willing to take constructive feedback from Step 2 and incorporate it into your Manuscript. You needn't use every critical comment provided, but it's best to approach this first round of critiques with an open mind. We've seen authors re-write entire chapters, and even entire Books, during this step. That's all right, though: if re-writing your Book is what it takes to make it the best it can be, then so be it. You want to be proud of your Book a year from now, ten years from now, don't you?

4. **Author Sends Manuscript to Content Editor**. Generally, the Content Editor is what most people think of when they think of Editors. Content Editors are the big-picture guys and gals who fine-tooth-comb your Manuscript for major errors, incongruities, and mistakes. They provide notes for how to make the Book better, how to make the story tighter, and how to improve things like plot, character development, structure, and dramatic arc. A solid Content Editor will save your Book from a stillbirth. If you're going to spend money on just one thing during the entire Publishing Process, it should be on a Content Editor. Find one you trust.

5. **Author Incorporates Content Editor's Feedback**. See #3. You want your Book to be great; thus, be willing to at least consider every suggestion. You may not use them all, but at least consider them. That way you know you've done your due diligence.

6. **Author Sends Manuscript to Copyeditor**. A quality Copyeditor (or two) will help the Author with the little stuff: grammatical errors, syntactical snafus, punctuation, stylistic quirks. For lack of a better characterization, a Copyeditor is a Professional Proofreader, which is sort of like a Mall Cop who's allowed carry a gun; he's not as serious as the real thing, but he can kill the bad guys when necessary.

7. **Author Incorporates Copyedits**. By now you're probably tired of reading your own book. We know. But remember: before you release it to the world you want it to be right, right? Right! Thankfully, the copyedits, though there will likely be many, are fairly objective (e.g., correcting spelling and punctuation and typos) and thus easy to incorporate into your Manuscript. Go slow. Take the time to fix your mistakes. Better now than after your Book is in print.

8. **Author Sends Manuscript to Final Proofreaders**. Remember those folks—family, friends, benevolent enemies—with whom you originally shared your Manuscript in Step 2? Well, it's time to ask them, or similar people you trust, to give your Book another once-over, a close look to find those handful of errors that inevitably remain. This's your final line of defense.

9. **Author Corrects Typos from Proofreaders**. Umm, Author corrects typos proofreaders bring to their attention. We all hat typos.

10. **Author Reads Manuscript One More Time**. No matter what, one or two typos'll always sneak by. The point isn't to produce a perfect, error-free Book; even masterpieces have a couple errors in their First Editions. The point, then, is to do the best you can do, to properly use all available resources so you can look yourself in the mirror and know that you owned every step of the Process. So go ahead—read that book one more time, fix whatever you can before you're ready to move to the next Part of the Process.

Yes, this is our actual Process. We didn't make it up just to write this essay; we really use it. Each step of the Process will have its own nuances: e.g., some Editors/Proofreaders will email you e-comments, while others prefer old-fashioned pen and paper. Etc. Etc. But the Process itself is a solid one, a proven one that has led to professional-quality Books for us time and again, books that are indistinguishable in quality from the Big Boys (commonly better than theirs, actually).

To put it bluntly, your Book, no matter how wonderful you think it is, needs to be thoroughly edited. More than anything else—more than even a Big Six logo on the dust jacket—editing will separate your work from the amateurs. Editing illuminates your Book's flaws so you can correct them before readers get a chance to sneer at them.

Whether you use our Process or some occult process you've devised on your own, make sure you don't skimp on this step. We're not fucking with you: don't skimp. We

want you to be successful; friends don't let frien
own work.

Further listening: Podcast: How to Edit a Book (http:// asymmetrical.co/?powerpress_pinw=1427-podcast)

CHAPTER 3: HOW TO CREATE A BOOK COVER, AUTHOR BIO, AND SYNOPSIS FOR YOUR BOOK

First Impressions

In life and in publishing, first impressions are vital. And when it comes to your Books, you have three major avenues through which to make that impression: your Cover, your Bio, and your Synopsis.

Your Cover is what potential readers will see sitting on bookstore shelves amid a clutter of other covers, or on the digital shelves, shrunk down to nothing, competing with everything else on the Internet (not a fair fight by any measure).

Your Bio is what they'll read when they want to know who you are and why they should read something you've written. *You* are your product, whether you're writing self-help or vampire fiction. That means you'd better have a Bio that quickly and accurately expresses who you are, giving them enough information to justify reading your words.

Your Synopsis is a summary of your Book, plain and simple. You need to touch on the important points and give away enough to tantalize without spoiling the major plot points or primary thesis. In essence, you have to give them a taste, but only a taste.

Saying Without Speaking: Your Book Cover

Your Book Cover is an opportunity to shout across a bookstore or through your computer at passersby, gripping them with dramatic imagery, compelling typography, or some other visual cue that they'll be attracted to. This attraction has as much to do with them as you, and as such, it's smart to take into account who your target audience is for the work. Romance novels shouldn't be covered with black and white Helvetica poetry, and punk-rock design Books shouldn't display (un-ironic) oil paintings of damsels riding white horses.

You have several options in getting an appropriate Cover designed for your Book, the first of which is to hire someone who knows how to do such things. Most print-on-demand services have some kind of Cover design add-on available (CreateSpace, for example, will do something professional[10] for somewhere between a few hundred to over a thousand dollars, depending on the complexity), and some also offer the option to build one yourself with an online tool they provide (again, CreateSpace has this option,[11] though the results tend to be what you would expect from a free service).

You can also find someone to design your Cover freelance for a very reasonable fee. The most common rates for well-designed work these days tend to be $200-1000, with most ending up in the $300-400 range. It's possible to find good work for less than that (at sites like 99Designs)[12], but it becomes a real gamble, and most of what's presented by crowdsourced schemes like that are templated or derivative (the designers doing the work can't afford to spend much time on the design because of the tiny amount they'll make for it). It's also possible to find work that costs more, but you should carefully calculate your expected returns on the Book ahead of time to make sure you aren't going over budget.

Another option is to learn to design your own book Covers. This may sound intimidating, and we won't tell you it's easy, but it is possible, and it could be a very viable option, especially if you plan on writing several books, or want to design books for other people, not just yourself. The first step to learning to design your own book Covers is learning the tools you'll use, and the most versatile tool you could have is Adobe Photoshop. You can pick up a whole lot about Photoshop online for free,[13] you can pay a monthly subscription to have access to premium tutorials,[14] or you can take a class like the one Colin teaches online (Intro to Design for Publishing)[15] and spend a month learning to design your own Covers, in addition to learning how to use the tools to communicate what you want to communicate.

Get to the Roots: Bio and Synopsis

Writing short pieces of work like **Bios and Synopses** is a deceptively difficult task. There's a quote by Antoine de Saint-Exupery that goes "A designer knows he has achieved perfection not when there is nothing left to add, but when there is nothing left to take away." The same is true with your Bio and summary. You want to tell the important things and nothing else. The tricky part is that what's important for one person or project won't necessarily be what's important for another.

When we write a Bio, we like to first consider our audience. In most cases the people you're trying to reach with a Bio are those who are unfamiliar with you or your work. As such, you don't want to use any inside jokes or sarcasm that might be misinterpreted. You should also be careful with humility or exaggeration. Think of your Bio the same way you would think of being introduced to a group of people by a friend—you don't want to have your traits or deeds blown way out of proportion, but you also don't want them to completely gloss over the points you would want others to know about you.

It also helps to divide up the information, if not into paragraphs (when space is an issue), then by sentence. Tell who you are and what you do. Then display some accolades (awards, press you've been mentioned in or shows you've been on, etc). Then tell something personal: where you're from, if you live with your family or your dog, things which help pull together who you are as a person and keep your Bio from seeming like an advertisement.

Your Synopsis works in much the same way as the Bio, though instead of writing about yourself, you're writing about your work. You want to keep it short and sweet, but your goal is to generate enough interest that someone reading the Synopsis will want to read more. You don't want to write in the same voice as the Book—instead you want to express in neutral words what value the Book presents, be it strong characters, a compelling storyline, or valuable insight into a certain field or practice. Paint a picture for the reader: with fiction, that will probably mean describing the main characters and the world they inhabit and conflicts they face. With nonfiction, you'll want to tell about the information or field you're discussing and the context in which you're discussing them (narrative, step-by-step, etc).

Being Prepared

For your Bio, Synopsis, and Cover, you'll want to have different versions to suite the myriad situations in which you'll need them.

When we publish a Book at Asymmetrical, we usually create at least three versions of each.

Author Bio Examples

We keep at least four sizes of Bio on hand for each author: snippets, small, medium, and large lengths.

The snippets are a sentence or two apiece, and focus on some aspect of the author. Here are two example snippets for Joshua Fields Millburn:

Snippet 1 (Fiction):

Joshua Fields Millburn is the author of eight books, including a novel As a Decade Fades *and the forthcoming story collection* Goodbye? *He lives in Montana.*

Snippet 2 (Nonfiction):

Joshua Fields Millburn is the author of eight books. He left his corporate career at age 30 to become a full-time author and writing instructor. His essays at TheMinimalists.com have garnered an audience of more than 100,000 monthly readers.

And here are examples of small, medium, and large Bios for JFM:

Small:

Joshua Fields Millburn left his corporate career at age 30 to become a full-time author and writing instructor. His essays at TheMinimalists.com have garnered an audience of more than 100,000 monthly readers. He has been featured on CBS This Morning, ABC, NBC, FOX, NPR, Wall Street Journal, USA Today, New York Times, Forbes, Elle Magazine, Boston Globe, and various other outlets.

Medium:

Joshua Fields Millburn jettisoned most of his material possessions and left his corporate career at age 30 to become a full-time author and writing instructor. His essays at TheMinimalists.com have garnered an audience of more than 100,000 monthly readers. He has published seven books, toured internationally, spoken at Harvard Business School, and has been featured on CBS This Morning, ABC, NBC, FOX, NPR, CBC Radio, Wall Street Journal, USA Today, New York Times, Forbes, Elle Magazine, Boston Globe, San Francisco Chronicle, San Francisco Examiner, Chicago Tribune, Chicago Sun-Times, Seattle Times, Toronto Star, Globe & Mail, Vancouver Sun, Village Voice, LA Weekly, Zen Habits, and various other outlets. He currently lives in Missoula, Montana. More info: JoshuaFieldsMillburn.com.

Large:

Joshua Fields Millburn left his corporate career at age 30 to become a full-time author and writing instructor. His essays at TheMinimalists.com have garnered an audience of more than 100,000 monthly readers.

Millburn is the bestselling author of three fiction and four nonfiction books and has been featured on CBS This Morning, ABC, NBC, FOX, NPR, CBC Radio, Wall Street Journal, USA Today, New York Times, Forbes, Elle Magazine, Boston Globe, San Francisco Chronicle, San Francisco Examiner, Chicago Tribune, Chicago Sun-Times, Seattle Times, Toronto Star, Globe & Mail, Vancouver Sun, Village Voice, LA Weekly, Zen Habits, and various other outlets.

He has toured internationally and has spoken at Harvard Business School, SXSW, World Domination Summit, and several other organizations, schools, and conferences.

In 2012, Millburn co-founded Asymmetrical Press, an independent publishing company and community that embraces new technologies, methods, and ideas to help writers and creators reach an audience.

Born in 1981 in Dayton, Ohio, Millburn currently lives in Missoula, Montana. Read more at his website, JoshuaFieldsMillburn.com.

Book Synopsis Examples

We usually write two main Synopses for the books we publish, one for use on sales platforms (like on Amazon), the other for longer description opportunities where people want to read more, rather than just getting the outline to decide whether or not they want to purchase it (pitches, blog posts, etc).

Here's a short sales Synopsis for Colin's book *Real Powers: Part One*:

It's 2027, and as the global economy shifts from unprecedented prosperity into harsh decline, the world's experts struggle to understand why.

A young blogger discovers a device with a hidden purpose, an idealistic journalist upends her career by targeting the people who own the news, a master media manipulator questions his work and takes on a challenging new client, an energy tycoon bristles as her powerful position is challenged, and a technologist-turned-cult leader questions his own faith.

The hacktivist group Opus makes headlines around the world—their intentions unclear—and spurred by events he doesn't fully understand, an unaccomplished young man born into a political dynasty decides to shatter conventions and expectations to take his rightful place in the world.

And a longer one, used in a pitch packet to generate interest in the series as a whole:

The year is 2027, and the world is a different place, though not different enough.

The global economy is on the verge of collapse, and although many claim the downswing is part of a natural cycle, there are others who think it's a harbinger of something much bigger. Of something orchestrated.

In Europe, the EU has been segmented into three classes, to make way for top-tier voting nations, non-voting union states, and third-tier debtor nations. The US is on the verge of a drone war with Canada over hotly contested Arctic mineral rights, and private corporations are beginning to flex their significant muscles, taking on entire governments in the pursuit of the most useful genetic technologies and other resources.

This is a world in which an asteroid the size of Michigan was detonated before it had the chance to strike the planet by a joint US/Brazilian effort called Occasio Ultima ('last chance') The remains of that asteroid were pulled into orbit around Earth and are now mined for rare earth minerals and other extra-planetary resources, leading to a land rush of sorts, and a wave of in-orbit industrialization that helped build careers and reputations.

A young tycoon named Niki Jenks emerged from the flurry of activity in the years after the asteroid. She built and conquered an entirely new industry, harvesting solar energy with a swarm of miniature satellites that could merge to form massive solar arrays, and then pull apart to deliver energy to nearby satellites and harvesting rigs through wireless inductive charging—the transmission of energy through antennas.

As the daughter of consumable resource energy tycoons, Niki carved out her own kingdom and expected to rule it, though the idea for the 'minilites' had come from someone else. Her ex-boyfriend, Mason.

Mason was a businessperson of the traditional sort, making his fortune online by producing valuable things and building communities around the people who wanted to buy them. After a few years of dating Niki, however, he found that his lifestyle no longer synced with his priorities, and he took off to travel full-time, leaving his former business endeavors—and his relationship with Niki—behind.

A cunning businessman, Mason was able to start new endeavors on the road, and it was one of these companies—an import/export business based in Argentina—that got him tangled up with something much larger than he could handle on his own.

While checking in on one of his warehouses in South America, he stumbled upon what seemed to be a robbery in progress, but which turned out to be a sleight of hand involving his warehouse space and a group of well-organized criminals. They seemed to have left behind a small, unextraordinary looking device of uncertain use, and that device pulled Mason into a conspiracy that would take him around the world, into a secret government prison facility, and back to the net, where he'd try to unravel the puzzle of what the device does, and what its creators intend to do with it.

But Mason isn't the only curious individual looking into the mystery of the devices and their faceless creators. Up-and-coming journalist Joanna Hubble caught the scent after being very publicly booted from her job with a well-respected news organization for looking into people who were above her pay grade—the monolithic Smith family of politicians and public officials, who also happened to be one of the largest investors in the organization.

The result of this firing was something she couldn't have predicted: fame. The world's most successful media-

manipulator—Manicule—identified her as the potential face of a movement, and made her past work a very public spectacle. Something that annoyed her to no end until she found her way to some people with answers, and those people helped her avoid not only the downsides of stardom, but of existing.

Joanna's disappearance threw a wrench in Manicule's plans, but he had others ways of pushing the new agenda he was championing—that of journalistic integrity—for his recent client, Michael Smith. Michael was a young, good-looking son of a family that was essentially American royalty, and as such was always competing with the exploits of his more successful siblings and other relatives. Catching himself at the bottom of a dangerous spiral, Michael decided to push himself for the first time ever and see what he could achieve; even if doing so went against his family's wishes.

Michael wasn't the only public figure taking a break from the status quo in order to make waves. Former technologist and current Singularity cult leader, Xerxes, found himself trying to staunch the flow of followers from his forward-facing organization —to where, he didn't know, but he intended to find out. After some research and following up on a surprisingly friendly, but still very threatening, letter, Xerxes worked to infiltrate the shadowy hacker collective known as 'Opus,' which was apparently the magnet pulling Xerxes' flock from his pastures. In doing so, he discovered that the group had made strides toward human/machine Singularity that he hadn't thought of, and decided that if they weren't going to take full public advantage of the technology they'd invented, he would.

*At the center of the tangled web is Opus—a g
news organizations liked to skewer, politicians liked
against, and governments loved to use as an excuse to pass
constricting laws—an organization that few know anything
about, other than that they brazenly deface and destroy that
which they find to be wrong and that their sigil—a colorful
wrestling mask that hearkens back to their early days taking
down cartels in Mexico—is the silence that appears before the
storm. An indication that something is going to change; and
that there's no way to stop it.*

And here's a nonfiction example from JFM's memoir *Everything That Remains*:

*Twenty-something, suit-clad, and upwardly mobile,
Joshua Fields Millburn thought he had everything anyone
could ever want.*

Until he didn't anymore.

*Blindsided by the loss of his mother and his marriage in
the same month, Millburn started questioning every aspect of
the life he had built for himself. Then, he accidentally
discovered a lifestyle known as minimalism…and everything
started to change.*

*That was four years ago. Since, Millburn, now 32, has
embraced simplicity. In the pursuit of looking for something
more substantial than compulsory consumption and the broken
American Dream, he jettisoned most of his material
possessions, paid off loads of crippling debt, and walked away
from his six-figure career.*

So. When everything was gone, what was left?

Everything That Remains *is the touching, surprising story of what happened when one young man decided to let go of everything and begin living more deliberately. Heartrending, uplifting, and deeply personal, this engrossing memoir is peppered with insightful (and often hilarious) interruptions by Ryan Nicodemus, Millburn's best friend of twenty years.*

Together, Millburn and Nicodemus co-founded TheMinimalists.com, a website with more than 2 million readers, where they write about living life with less money, less stuff, and more meaningfulness. Their story has been featured on CBS This Morning, ABC, NBC, FOX, NPR, CBC Radio, Wall Street Journal, USA Today, Forbes, Elle Canada, Boston Globe, San Francisco Chronicle, San Francisco Examiner, Chicago Tribune, Chicago Sun-Times, Austin American-Statesman, Seattle Times, Toronto Star, Globe & Mail, National Post, Vancouver Sun, LA Weekly, Zen Habits, and numerous other outlets.

(Note: Because it's often difficult for Authors to coherently condense their work into something more soundbite-ish, Joshua hired a professional copywriter to write his book's synopsis. This is advisable if you need a clean pair of eyes to distill your book down to its essence.)

Promo Graphics

You'll want a few different version of your Book Cover for promotional purposes, allowing for different sizes, some with words, some without, often reusing colors and elements so that they will be recognizable even when used as banners or posters.

Here are some examples from *Real Powers: Part One*:

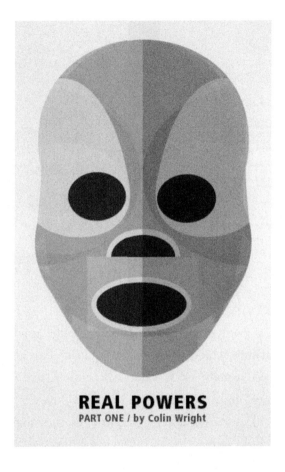

The above image is an ebook Cover, sized to Amazon's specifications (you might tweak it for other platforms, but most will accept this sizing standard, as well).

Above is a print-ready Cover/spine/back file, used for the print version, which we use in addition to an ebook version. We usually use CreateSpace, and as such use their file settings, but[16] you'll want to make sure to create a different file for each service you use, as the smallest size changes could make a huge difference in how the finished product looks.

Above's a banner created for the Real Powers series, incorporating imagery from the second book's Cover as well. This kind of banner is used as more of a tease, and is best utilized when the imagery is strong, so that you needn't use text to draw attention to it.

REAL POWERS
PART ONE / by Colin Wright

Above: you can create side banner quite easily by rearranging the elements from your Cover. Another option is to write up a super-brief Synopsis or callout about the book, and use it alongside an element from the Cover (image, title, colors, etc).

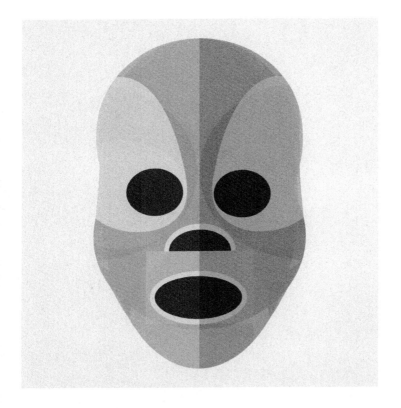

Finally, we used the above icon for the social media accounts for the series. Simple, no text (some networks don't allow too much text in your avatar photo), and distinctive.

Further listening: Podcast: Covers, Bios, and Synopses (http://asymmetrical.co/?powerpress_pinw=1503-podcast)

CHAPTER 4: HOW TO FORMAT YOUR BOOK FOR PRINT, EBOOK, AND AUDIOBOOK

The Beauty and the Books

Bookstores are beautiful places. Walk into any well-curated Indie Bookshop and it's like being welcomed home, hugged by millions of pages of text. This beauty, however, is not accidental. Rather, it's an intentional, sensuous experience: that in-awe feeling we experience from Books is one part kinesthetic (the feel of touching/turning the pages), one part olfactory (the smell that overtakes you when you first enter a Bookstore), and one part visual.

The latter part has something to do with the Book cover, at least at first glance, but the overall visual experience can be mostly attributed to how the Books are laid out—that is, how well they are formatted.

Hence, We have some enjoyable homework for you...

Praxis: Spend some time in a Bookstore this week. (Bring a ruler.) Go first to all the Books you usually gravitate toward. Inspect them closely. What about them attracts your attention? Which books do you pick up and thumb through? Which Books do you ignore altogether? Why? Is it the cover? The size? The thickness? The paper? Spend time really looking at each Book, even the Books you'd likely never pick up: Does the typeface look proportionate? Is the kerning[17] just right? How about the margins—what are their measurements? Measure the size of the Book—is it 5"x8", 6"x9", something else?

You'll start to notice that every Book is different, even the beautiful, well-formatted ones—each one different in myriad ways. Like a delicate snowflake or some other cheesy metaphor that barely makes sense.

At first, this fact might frustrate you. It sure as hell frustrated us: *Why the hell don't publishers have standard sizes? What's the formula?* But there is no formula, and so we have to go with our proverbial guts when formatting our Books.

Types of Books

Let's talk about the three Types of Books you'll (likely) want to format for (noting, of course, that each Type has several sub-Types; e.g., "Ebooks" contains sub-Types Kindle, Nook, and so forth).

1. **Print Books**. Even though we've already talk about What the Hell a Book Is in Chapter One, it's true that many of us still think of Books in the traditional sense of the word: i.e., a printed work consisting of pages glued or sewn together along one side and bound in covers. Thus, when approaching formatting for your book, Print Books are a good place to start. If you're printing a Book containing mostly text, then the best software to use is Scrivener (more on software below). It's important to realize that formatting is a tedious process, especially at first, while you're learning; it's a process that requires hours of adjusting and tweaking and re-adjusting/tweaking until you have a product you're happy with. But it's totally worth it. You want to be happy with/proud of your Book, and spending hours getting it right will ensure a level of quality with which you can be happy.

Specs: irrespective of a Book's length (it can be 58 pages or 300), we tend to use the following specifications when formatting for print:

- **Page/Book Size**: 5"x8". This is the most common size used in trade paperback publishing (6"x9" is also popular for some Books), and we've found it to be the perfect size for most of our Books. Also, it's the smallest non-custom size offered by CreateSpace and other printers.
- **Font/Typeface**: We like Garamond and its derivates for our Print Books. We've also used Minion, Caslon, and Georgia in the past, all of which are beautiful serif fonts that work well in print. The font size of our

Books varies a bit, but not much, and it usually ends up around size 11 (occasionally we'll go as low as 10.7 or as high as 11.2, but no farther, unless it's the copyright page, which we usually set in size 9 font).

• **Front Matter**: all the stuff that's at the beginning of a book is important: the title page, bastard title page,[18] copyright page, dedication, epigraph, table of contents, etc., all of which are somewhat optional in that you get to chose how and where to place them. But remember: you want this stuff there; it adds a perceived legitimacy to your Book and also gives readers a chance to learn a little more about the book if interested. At Asymmetrical we almost always hide something funny or obscene on the copyright page for our attentive readers. (Hence, you can have fun with even the most tedious aspects of formatting.) When creating the front matter for our Books, we'll often look through stacks of Books at an Indie Bookstore to find the content we like most and then emulate it using our own ingredients.

• **End Matter**: After the Book's content—i.e., the meat of your book, its chapters and words, the meaningful stuff—usually comes at least three different bits of end matter: 1) Acknowledgements page, where you thank the folks you want to thank; 2) About the Author Page, which'll include your black and white photo and bio; and 3) Other Books by This Author, which is nice if you have other Books in print.

2. **Ebooks**. Once your Print Book is formatted, it's time to move on to the wide array of Ebooks. This format covers any and all e-, ahem, *electronic* Books: Kindle, Kobo, Nook, Sony e-reader, and any other e-reader-esque device, including devices that use e-reader apps, such as the free Kindle App that works on PCs, Macs, iPads, tablets, iPhones, Androids, and BlackBerrys.

While we still enjoy the sensuous experience of physical books, much of our reading these days is done on some sort of device (*viz.* a Kindle or the Kindle app on a phone). What we've discovered is that the sensuousness of the experience is still there in Ebooks; it just manifests differently. Thus, formatting your Book well for Ebook is just as important as formatting for Print.

This is often where Big Six Publishers, as well as small publishing houses and Indie Authors, go wrong—a fatal mistake. Spend time formatting your Ebook (see tools/Software below), because in the long run, you'll likely sell more Ebooks than Print Books. Nothing makes someone "put down" an Ebook quicker than bad formatting.

Like Print Books, it's best to understand what you're looking for in terms of formatting—what looks good, what doesn't—which means dutifully looking at many other Ebooks on multiple devices (Kindle, Kindle App, iBooks, etc.) to discover what works and what doesn't work. Model the stuff that works; throw out the rest.

3. **Audiobooks**. Don't sleep on Audiobooks. As technology improves, Audiobooks' share of the pie continues to

increase more than any other Type. Some Indie Authors cover their rent/mortgage from Audiobook sales these days, a feat we'd've thought impossible two years ago. At the moment, the best way to get your Audiobook to the masses is via ACX (more on ACX in Chapter 5), but before you can sell your high-quality Audiobook, you have to create it.

Formatting Software

1. **Scrivener**. If there is a such thing as a must-have Software for writers, it's Scrivener, which not only allows you to keep your work organized—chapters, characters, sections, notes, etc.—it also allows you to format for Print Books and all different Types of Ebooks. Like anything new, it takes some getting used to, but it's worth the learning curve. Oh, and it's relatively inexpensive (less than $50). Check out Colin Wright's Beginner's Guide to Using Scrivener[19] for more details, including a video tutorial, screenshots, instructions, and an Asym Community discussion.

2. **InDesign**. While Scrivener is the multi-purpose workhorse built with the work of ebooks and text-focused print books in mind, InDesign is the fuller-featured next step up, adding more features than you would believe and nearly unlimited options when it comes to layout and image presentation—two things that Scrivener lacks. That

being said, InDesign is so powerful that most people will never use more than a very small fraction of what it offers, which is why it's best saved for specific types of projects. Newspapers, magazines, coffee table books, books on design or art or other subjects that require lots of visuals—this is InDesign's domain, and it does the work incredibly well. The learning curve is steep, especially if you've never used Adobe products or layout software before, but it's very much worth the time and effort if you are looking for the largest possible number of options when publishing and want more control over how your work—text and imagery—is presented.

3. **Misc. & Meat Grinders**. Some platforms give authors the option of uploading their finished manuscript in any format, including a Word document. Smashwords, for example, will allow you to upload just about anything and then push that file through their 'Meat Grinder' software, which converts it into the various formats necessary to publish on the main publishing platforms (.epub and .mobi). This is a nice option to have, and frankly it's really helped reduce the number of hurdles between a first-time author and publication, but it also has the unfortunate side effect of creating truly horrible looking ebooks. A quick online search will net you many horror stories of a beautiful piece of work rendered all but unreadable after being filtered through the Meat Grinder, and similar software on other sites doesn't fare much better in the court of public opinion. Nook Press has stepped up their game

by allowing you to upload your file and then edit it on their in-site software (which works a lot like Scrivener, though a stripped-down version), which helps alleviate the worst of the damage, but in general it's best to avoid this kind of process if you're looking to produce high-quality work from your high-quality words.

4. **Adobe Audition** (Audiobooks). Like InDesign, Audition is a part of the Adobe family of software, which means that it's pro-level kit intended for folks who take their work seriously. The learning curve can be steep, and although there are a massive number of free tutorials and documentation available, it's not something you can open up and start using right out the door—not unless you have experience with other audio software, at least. Again, like InDesign, Audition has more features than someone wanting to record an audiobook will ever use, but it also has some extremely high-quality features that are difficult to find in more consumer-grade software (things like on-the-fly filtering, EQ-adjustment, and adaptive noise-reduction. Audition (or other pro-level software, like Logic Pro), when paired with the right hardware, is what makes the difference between something that sounds pretty good for being done at home, and something that sounds really, really good, period. If you're looking for an open source alternative, try Audacity, though be warned that it doesn't have a fraction of a percentage of the capabilities boasted by Audition. It's a good place to start, though, if you're unsure of how much you want to

commit to recording and producing your own audiobooks.

Hiring Someone to Format

Formatting can seem overwhelming—trust us, we know. But learning the Software and the skills required to format your own Book will help immensely in the long run. That being said, while we were first learning how to format our Books, we hired someone to do the formatting for us. Ergo, if it makes you feel better, you can ask someone you trust to do the same while you're learning. Asymmetrical offers access to talented, affordable formatters in our Studio, available at http://asymmetrical.co/services

Further listening: Podcast: How to Format Your Book (http:// asymmetrical.co/?powerpress_pinw=1559-podcast)

CHAPTER 5: HOW TO DISTRIBUTE YOUR BOOK

Shelves and E-Shelves

Living in the future as we do, we're fortunate to have many, many options when it comes to publishing written work that we've lovingly produced. The downside of this is that there are so many options available, it can be difficult to distinguish between them, leaving many people scrambling to differentiate between all the alternatives, often with sub-optimal results.

But fear not! Herein we will endeavor to not only explain the difference between the options you have available, but also help you determine which of the options is best for you, your project, and the eventual readers/listeners/consumers of your work.

General Considerations

The first thing you'll want to figure out is what format or formats you'll be utilizing.

The three main options here are: ebook, paperback, and audiobook. There are a few other options, and we'll talk about them at the end of this chapter, but 99% of the work produced and published ends up as one of these three main formats.

Within those formats, there are other sub-options to consider.

When it comes to ebooks, you'll need to determine which file type to make use of, and this decision will hinge on the online sales platform you decide on. This will be partially determined by the type of book (novella, picture book, cookbook), and partially by the type of customer you'll be selling to (luddites might prefer Kindle because it works seamlessly, for example, while books written for programmers could be published on a website or more open format).

Paperback books also have many sub-options to consider, from the size of the book (width, height) to the type of paper (glossy, matte, white, off-white) to the method of binding (perfect, saddle-stitch, ring-bound).

Audiobooks are less complicated in that the general standards apply across the board, but are more complex in that the minute details of the file you submit, and the standard prices you're able to charge for your work, change from platform to platform.

But enough of the generalities, let's dig in to each of these groups individually.

Online

One of the most exciting aspects of being an author or publisher today is the opportunities afforded by the so-called ebook revolution. Now that a significant number of people have ebook reader devices or software on their phones and computers, the ebook market has grown ambitiously year after year, rattling the nerves of some players in the industry and sparking a fire for others.

For you, independently publishing your work will very likely include some kind of ebook, because there's little reason not to. The cost of operation is essentially zero (literally zero, after the product is finished), so once you've written the book and produced it to perfection, popping it up on one of the myriad ebook shops is a piece of cake and something you'll never have to touch again, if you prefer.

Regardless of your format, you will need to procure an ISBN for your book(s). ISBN stands for International Standard Book Number. It's basically your book's unique serial number. ISBNs are linked to essential information allowing booksellers and readers to know what book they are buying, what the book is about, and who the author is.

At Asymmetrical we use two ISBN's for each of our books: one for ebook and another for print (either ISBN will work for the audiobook version of your book, which does not require a separate ISBN). ISBNs are cheapest if you buy them in bulk directly from Bowker.[20] If you don't think you'll need more than one (or two, since you'll need one for your ebook and one for your paperback edition), you might consider buying from a reseller, rather than forking over a lot of money for just a few.

You'll also need to make sure your book is in the proper format for the platform you're using. Browse through the list of platforms below, and you'll see we've specified the format you'll need for each one, along with other considerations you'll need to keep in mind when choosing between them.

Online Platforms

Platforms sell your books through their own distribution networks—much like a traditional bookstore, but instead of being limited to a few shops, their storefront is anywhere their websites and apps can be accessed. **Distributors** will take your book (and often help you convert it to the proper format) and distribute it to many different platforms, usually leaving the selling to others, though they may help you manage your visibility.

Amazon's Kindle

The 800-pound gorilla in the room, Amazon's Kindle is the dominant player in the ebook world, far outdistancing even its closest competitors in both variety of books available and sales of those books.

Amazon's strengths here are two-fold. The first is that they have an incredibly well-known online footprint, and there's a chance that someone shopping on their site for socks will also pick up your book. The second is that they have the most popular ereader device on the market (the Kindle), which has become an eponymous title for ereaders as a whole (like 'Kleenex' or 'Xerox' in their respective fields, 'Kindle' is another way to say 'ebook reader device').

In order to get your book on the Kindle store, you'll need a .mobi file, a cover (1563 x 2500 pixels is ideal), and a KDP account. From there you can submit your book, which point will take anywhere from a handful of hours to a few days to show up on Amazon.com. In the meantime, you'll be able to flesh out your Amazon presence by creating an author profile at their Author Central page.

The process will be slightly different if you're opting to produce work in Amazon's proprietary KF8 format, which is their spin on EPUB3, and allows you to produce work that is more interactive and colorful, utilizing the power of HTML5 and CSS3 (in essence, this means you can more easily fix the layout of your books, use color, create children's books, and produce graphic novels for the Kindle ecosystem). The downside is that KF8 books will only work on Kindle Fire readers or other color-enabled ebook readers with Kindle software installed. The KindleGen software[21] is also a lot less developed and intuitive than Apple's iBooks Producer software (discussed below).

Basics:

- Start here: https://kdp.amazon.com/signin
- Formats accepted: .mobi, Word (.doc or .docx), HTML, .epub, .txt, .rtf, .pdf. Format recommended: .mobi (any other format will be converted into .mobi, potentially ruining any formatting work you've done), or .KF8 for image-heavy books
- Royalties: 35% or 70%, depending on the country you're selling in and the price of your book (the 70% option is only available in select countries, and for others is only available if you're a part of KDP Select[22] — the cost of delivering the file is subtracted from your royalty, so this option is best for books with smaller file sizes, and you can only choose 70% if your book costs between $2.99 and $9.99 USD). Payout is via check, or through Amazon Payments[23] (which is a lot like Paypal), each month

Pros:

- Largest library, largest audience
- Best name recognition
- Interesting programs like Kindle Owner's Lending Library, Kindle Singles, and Whispersync (which allows readers to switch between the written and audiobook versions of a book seamlessly).
- Fairly simple registration and submission process

Cons:

- All the downsides that come with being just a tiny snowflake inside a blizzard of ebook authors
- Amazon will sometimes cut the prices on your books without warning, or do other strange things like that
- Amazon Payments is not as ubiquitous as Paypal, so getting paid if you're outside the US or another major international market can be tricky
- Books are locked in Amazon's ecosystem, and the deeper you get, the less freedom you'll have to deal with other platforms

Barnes & Noble's Nook

The Nook is—in many ways—the Pepsi to Kindle's Coca-

Cola. Depending on who you ask and when, either Nook or Apple's iBooks are second place in the ebook market. Second place isn't a terrible spot to hold, however, as it's given the Nook team a chance to innovate in small ways, and just like the aforementioned soft drink comparison, the Nook has managed to gain some die-hard fans as a result.

The biggest difference between publishing on the Nook (using Nook Press) and publishing through Amazon's Kindle platform is that while Kindle allows you to upload a document to be converted to the proper format, the Nook platform allows you to build your book inside their platform. That means the tools you would normally use (like Scrivener) to publish your ebook file wouldn't be necessary; you could do all of your layout work on the Nook Press site itself. There are a few other minor differences—the royalty structure is staggered differently from the Kindle's, for example—but the main differences are purely brand oriented.

Basics:

- Start here: https://www.nookpress.com
- Formats accepted: .epub, .pdf, .txt, .rtf. Format recommended: using their built-in editor will probably garner the best results
- Royalties: 65% for books $2.99 to $9.99, 40% for all other price points (an advantage over Kindle's method is that you don't pay for the delivery of the file to the reader's device)

Pros:

- Seems to be focusing on work from indie authors, which could mean more promotion in the future
- Slightly better royalties if your work falls outside the $2.99 - $9.99 price range
- Books are saved as .epub files, which many people prefer over the .mobi files Kindles use (which is a latent type of DRM, even if you don't want any DRM on your books), and which means you're less locked in to their ecosystem
- Better book-publishing experience—very simple compared to Amazon's somewhat-simple process
- Publishing software baked in to the platform, making it a one-stop production and publishing resource, if you wish to use it that way

Cons:

- Much smaller audience, and far fewer Nook devices in the wild
- Fewer options beyond the standard store compared to Kindle

iBooks

The iBooks store is a large platform and brings a lot to the table, but also has many limitations.

First and foremost among its limitations is that you cannot read any of the books published on this platform unless you're using the approved Apple app, and that app is only available for the iPhone, iPod Touch, iPad, and Mac through the iTunes store.

Second is that the process of publishing a book on the service is famously difficult. In theory it should be quite simple, because it makes use of proprietary desktop apps instead of web apps to publish the book and mange your account, and proprietary formats for the books themselves. But despite all this customization, you'll still need to download iBooks Author[24] to produce and upload the book. If you use some other software to produce the ebook file, you'll need iTunes Producer to upload it to the iBooks store. The not-entirely-surprising kicker? You'll need an Apple computer to use iBooks Author and iTunes Producer. Tough luck if you're on anything else.

All that said, iBooks is still a top contender as a platform for two main reasons: the growing ubiquity of Apple products (and their 'it just works' mantra, which encourages owners of said devices to use Apple software like iBooks), and the wonderful way iBooks displays books that are heavy on images and other media. Additionally, Apple's focus on education means the tools available for producing and publishing digital textbooks are second to none.

Basics:

- Start here: http://www.apple.com/itunes/working-itunes/sell-content/
- Formats accepted: only .epub and their own proprietary .ibooks format, though you can output from iBooks Author as an .epub or .pdf, and use those files elsewhere
- Royalties: 70%, no muss, no fuss

Pros:

- For people who are targeting an Apple device-using audience, and who themselves use Apple computers, and who are producing work with images, videos, or anything beyond text, it's the single best platform available
- Building a media-rich book is easy as can be using the iBooks Author app
- iTunes U[25] is an interesting opportunity for textbooks and book-driven courses
- Allows you to set your book prices to 'Free' at any time
- 70% royalty applies at any price point (though they do limit you to certain pricing options)

Cons:

- Only available to readers with the correct iOS or OS X devices
- Sub-optimal reading experience, compared to other offerings (Kindle, Nook, and Kobo apps, not to mention ebook readers themselves)

Kobo

Although it possesses an ebook market share in the low single digits in the US, Kobo has ebook markets in over 190 countries and is dominant in many of them, including Canada, France, South Africa, and New Zealand. In many countries around the world, Kobo is the *only* player in the ebook game, and as such it's proving to be quite the contender, despite being an also-ran in some of the larger markets.

Basics:

- Start here: https://www.kobo.com/writinglife
- Formats accepted: .epub, .doc, .docx, .mobi, .odt. Recommended format: .epub (otherwise, their software will convert your file into an .epub, and you may not like the formatting changes made)
- Royalties: 70% on books between $1.99 and $12.99, 45% on books above or below that price range

Pros:

- Attractive and intuitive author dashboard and publishing process
- Allows you to set your book prices to 'Free' at any time
- Better royalties on a larger number of price points
- Massive international presence
- Android, iPhone/iPod/iPad, Mac/PC app for reading and shopping for ebooks

Cons:

- Pays out royalties only twice a year, unless your sales reach a certain minimum threshold
- Many international markets won't be interested in books not published in their native language
- Large number of ebook readers sold, but not as many ebooks as would be expected

Google Play Books

Technically, Google Play Books is the world's largest online bookstore, with over 4 million ebooks, but it has only 1-2% of the marketshare. Books purchased through Google Play Books can be read via an app on Android and iOS devices, as well as in Google's Chrome browser.

A feature unique to Google Play is the option to

download books either as an .epub or as a fixed-layout PDF, depending on which format(s) the publisher provides, although books downloaded as a PDF can be difficult to read on devices with small screens.

Basics:

- Start here: https://play.google.com/books/publish/
- Formats accepted: .pdf and .epub
- Royalties: Difficult to determine based on Google's documentation

Pros:

- Searchability is Google's forte
- Books can be downloaded as an .epub or, if the publisher provides one, as a fixed-layout PDF, meaning books can be read in their original layout

Cons:

- Uploading files to Google Play can be a difficult process, and little documentation exists to provide assistance. In fact, little documentation exists with regard to any aspect of Google Play Books, including royalties.

Smashwords

Smashwords is an underdog in that it's less of an ecosystem than the above platforms, and serves as both platform (books are available through the Smashwords store) and distributor (you can publish through Smashwords to Amazon, iBooks, Nook, Kobo, and other platforms).

The Smashwords platform is well-known for hosting a few main genres: romance books, mysteries, and thrillers. Other types of books are available, but these three seem to fare better than any of the others, and as a result (or maybe the other way around), many of the readers and authors who swear by the site and its offerings are producers and consumers of those genres of fiction. That's an advantage to some, and for others the higher royalty rate for authors, coupon generator, and ease of distribution might be a tempting selling point.

That said, Smashwords has far fewer books on hand and is not built natively into any app (Kindle, Nook, and iBooks can all sell books at the tap of a finger on an ebook reader smartphone screen, while those who wish to purchase from Smashwords have to visit the website, create an account, and jump through a few other hoops to get satisfaction). It doesn't have the strongest ecosystem of the platforms available, but it's certainly the largest and most well-known apart from the big four listed above.

Basics:

- Start here: http://www.smashwords.com/about/how_to_publish_on_smashwords
- Formats accepted: .doc and .epub. Format preferred: both work equally well, providing that they adhere to Smashwords' fairly rigid style guide, though the .epub file presumably undergoes less transformation when put through the Meat Grinder than the .doc file, so that would be preferred.
- Royalties: authors earn 70.5 - 85% from ebooks sold through Smashwords platform, 60% from sales on other platforms where they distribute your work

Pros:

- 'Meat Grinder' software can convert a .doc Word file into functional ebook files
- Functions as both platform and distributor, saving you time if you want to put your book up for sale across multiple platforms
- Potentially higher royalty rates, especially at lower and higher price points
- Coupon generator, allowing for free books as giveaways, buy-one-get-one deals, and the like

Cons:

- Ebook files produced by Meat Grinder are godawful ugly and unprofessional looking
- As a platform, lacks audience and ease-of-use others bring to the table

Lulu

Better known for their book printing services, Lulu also has dipped their toes into the world of ebook publishing with their platform, the Lulu Marketplace.

The main differentiator between Lulu and the platforms listed above is that foot traffic to the Lulu Marketplace is nearly nonexistent—there's a chance someone could stumble upon your book randomly while searching for some phrase or another, but it wasn't built to be an Amazon competitor, it was built to give people who publish through them a store from which to sell to their existing audience (friends, family, readers). This results in the highest royalty of any platform, but a 'bring your own ball' approach to selling your work.

Like Smashwords, Lulu also operates as a distributor to other platforms, though it gives fewer options in that department. It does, however, have a well known paperback printing department, which gives it an advantage over most other platforms.

Basics:

- Start here: http://www.lulu.com/publish/ebooks/
- Formats accepted: .epub, .doc, .docx, or .rtf. Preferred format: .epub (anything else may result in sub-par layout changes)
- Royalties: 90% of retail price when sold from their platform, varies when sold on partner marketplaces

Pros:

- Platform and distributor
- Also allows you to sell printed editions of your book
- High royalty compared to other platforms

Cons:

- No real audience to sell to, beyond what you bring with you
- Converter tends to shred ebook formatting if you use anything except an .epub

Other Online Options

Although selling through platforms and distributors makes sense for many people—especially when just starting out—

there are also options for those who want an online hub but don't want to be limited by the marketplace their work is sold through.

In this case, you might consider platformless, self-managed online sales services. Some are free and take a small cut of the sale, others require a monthly payment, but leave you to make as much money as you can once that flat fee is covered.

e-junkie

A long-time heavyweight of online sales, e-junkie's proposition is simple. You sign up and pay a fixed amount per month, and from there you can sell as many products as you want (up to the limit for your price bracket) to as many people as you want. They don't take any fees above and beyond the monthly payment, so you're good to expand and charge what you want. e-junkie has long been a favorite among the online marketing and blogging caste, too, because it allows for affiliates (where others can sign up to help sell your books, and then take a cut of the profit for each sale they bring in), discount codes, and other useful features.

Basics:

- Start here: http://www.e-junkie.com/ej/features.htm

- $5/month to $265/month, depending on number of products and storage space allotted (you can host your files on your own server, but the ability to do so will cost you)
- You sell on any site using their buttons and banners and URLs, and manage everything from a centralized dashboard
- Only for the technology-savvy—it's not rocket science to learn, but it's not easy, either

Pros:

- Easy to set up affiliate programs, promotions, and other advanced marketing gimmickry
- Quite cheap (flat fee), especially if you're selling a lot of books
- Been around a long time, so quite reliable

Cons:

- A bit outdated, in looks and technology
- Sometimes their delivery emails (sending ebooks to the buyers) end up in Spam folder

Gumroad

Ultra-simple and minimal, Gumroad was built in response to the more feature-filled and convoluted online shopping carts that came before. All you have to do is sign up, fill out a couple of fields and upload your product, and then share the link (or embed the code) it gives you. There's also a bit of analytics and such, but it's quite minimal. One of the simpler ways to sell something, if you don't mind paying for the service with a cut of the action, and only selling to your existing audience (since there is no platform involved except your own).

Basics:

- Start here: https://gumroad.com
- Costs 5% of item price plus $.25 per transaction
- Provides a URL and embeddable code (for use on your website/blog) which displays your sale page

Pros:

- Incredibly simple to set up and use—takes all of a minute or two to get going
- Relatively cheap for the service it provides
- One of the first of its ilk, so probably not going anywhere

Cons:

- Lacks any features beyond the bare bones basics
- If you're looking to sell to people outside of your existing network, look elsewhere

WooCommerce / Squarespace Commerce

WooCommerce is a very sophisticated *free* plugin for Wordpress that turns your blog or website into a fully-functioning e-commerce store. It's very feature-rich right out of the box, and if you find something it can't do, you'll very likely be able to remedy that situation by purchasing an extension (everything from drag-and-drop shopping cart experiences to accepting Bitcoin payments).

You can buy WooCommerce solo and add it to your existing Wordpress setup, or you can buy it in tandem with a specialized theme that was made with the plugin in mind. Either way, it's a really rugged setup with a lot of bells and whistles, capable of selling e-goods, physical goods, and even subscriptions.

Similarly, Squarespace is a blogging platform with a built-in Commerce app,[26] which—because it's a walled garden, as opposed to Wordpress' freewheeling open source status—is well integrated across their entire catalog of templates, and requires less fiddling to fix otherwise-inevitable glitches and display issues. The downside is that Squarespace will cost you ($30/month if you want to use their Commerce offerings, or $24/month if you pay a year in advance), which could be a deal-breaker for some. That being said, if the monthly cost doesn't faze you (and if you appreciate that they don't take any additional fees for using their platform, above the cost of the integrated credit card processor), it's a great option that's easy to set up and go. They also have famously solid customer service, so some hand-holding is available, which isn't typically the case with a Wordpress/WooCommerce combo.

Basics:

- Start here: http://www.woothemes.com/woocommerce/
- Free, but extensions will cost you $99 and up, and themes are about the same
- Works within a website you set up, but also capable of allowing you to advertise elsewhere, pulling people back to the main site

Pros:

- Very active community, so if you run into a problem, there's likely a solution available
- You really can accomplish just about anything you want, from building premium online courses to selling ebooks to building packages of products and selling them at a discounted rate

Cons:

- Might be a little *too* feature-rich if you're simply looking to sell a few ebooks
- Some solutions require programming knowledge to apply, and the people who built WooCommerce are not always polite in dealing with luddites

- Price of extensions can really add up, if you're looking to do something specialized with your shop

Paypal / Amazon Payments / Google Wallet

Sometimes the simple answers are the best ones, and if you're looking for a quick and easy way to sell online, and not concerned about scaling and automating your operation right away, using a straight-up payment gateway might be the right option.

A payment gateway, pure and simple, allows you to receive money online. You provide a link or a shopping cart button, someone else clicks it and says what product they're purchasing, and then they pay you using credit they have on that particular gateway, or a credit card they enter when checking out. That money then resides in your gateway account until you pull it out, either by using the account to buy something else online, or by transferring it into your bank account.

Basics:

- Start here for Paypal: https://www.paypal.com
- Start here for Amazon Payments: https://payments.amazon.com/home
- Start here for Google Wallet: https://www.google.com/wallet
- Super-simple, and three legit options from major players in the field

- You can build a button and embed the link on your website, or just have people send a specific amount of money to your account
- All three will take a cut of the sale as payment, plus a small fee on top of that cut—the percentages differ minutely
- The main difference between the three is that Paypal is the most well-known and commonly used, while Google Wallet and Amazon take slightly smaller fees per transaction, and don't work in every country

Pros:

- Keeps things simple
- No middle man between you and the money exchange, and easy to pull your money out to your bank afterward

Cons:

- Doesn't scale well—it's hard to keep track of who you need to email an ebook to after they've paid
- Not terribly professional or slick, if you're into that kind of thing
- Could be too simple, if you're trying to do anything beyond "You send me money, I give you book" transactions

Audiobooks

There are far fewer options when it comes to publishing and selling audiobooks online, but thankfully the few that exist are decent enough to make what used to be a fairly obtuse industry (when audiobooks only existed as mountains of cassettes or CDs) quite accessible.

ACX

The best known distributor for audiobooks is ACX, which will take your work and distribute it to the three main platforms: Amazon, Audible, and iTunes (the three biggest players in the online audiobook scene—though Audible is also owned by Amazon, so you could say there are only two main platforms, though they still maintain a brand distinction).

ACX is interesting in that it also helps you create an audiobook, should you wish to take that route. You can post your work to their site and narrators will submit an example of what they have to offer if they're interested in taking on the project. In return, you'll either pay them (if they're more experienced, this is more common), or they'll take a cut of each sale (more common if they're new to the industry). This is a great option if you're not really interested in doing any of the leg-work to get an audiobook made but want to have one available, as it's very hands-off for you.

The alternative is producing your own audiobook files, which you then upload to ACX for them to review. After the review process (which can take upwards of a month, be warned) your book will be made available on the three platforms mentioned above—on Amazon, it will be listed alongside your ebook and/or paperback offerings.

Note that you don't get to choose your own price when you go through ACX—they decide based on the duration of the ebook. This isn't the end of the world in most cases, but if you're hoping for free reign over such things, you might be better off producing an audiobook and then selling the file through a platform like e-junkie or Gumroad.

Basics:

- Start here: http://www.acx.com/help/how-it-works/200484210
- Distributes to the three major audiobook platforms: Amazon, Audible, and iTunes
- Also serves as a matchmaker between authors and narrators

Pros:

- Fairly easy to use, so long as you have a basic knowledge of audio production (if you want to create your own audiobook), very easy to use if you want to have someone else handle the production angle

- Simple way to get an audiobook made for little or no upfront investment
- Hands-off distribution to the main audiobook markets, and excellent integration with Amazon's offerings

Cons:

- Little choice in pricing of your work
- Can be a bit confusing at first if your experience with online sales platforms is limited
- You can't submit your audiobook file for review until you've published an ebook or paperback version on Amazon (and then the review takes up to a month or longer), making a synchronized launch nearly impossible

Print Platforms

Ebooks are the new kid in town that everyone wants to meet, but printed books are still selling well and in some genres will remain dominant long into the future. Thankfully, there are print on demand (POD) services available to authors who want the ease of production and sales that ebooks offer, while still providing a tangible finished product that you can sign, sell, and see on bookshelves, unlike their ebook brethren.

CreateSpace

CreateSpace is, like Amazon, a dominant force in the POD world. Which makes sense, as it is owned by Amazon, and integrated fairly well into their overall offerings.

As a result, CreateSpace has become the platform of choice among online authors wanting to hit a real-world audience with their words, and the former number one (Lightning Source) has taken a back seat, though CreateSpace still lags behind its rival in a few key ways. The first is selection of print options: Lightning Source allows for a wider range of trim sizes and the option to print hardcover books. It also allows for limited print runs instead of just POD (which means you'll get a discount if you print 50 or more books at a time—an amazing deal, since most print companies require 1,500 copies to be ordered minimum before you can even think of doing a print run), something that CreateSpace doesn't offer.

Lightning Source also allows you to accept returns from bookstores, though given the likelihood that a bookstore will stock an indie book without having a preexisting relationship with you (incredibly unlikely), that's not a major deal-breaker.

For its part, CreateSpace is the cheaper option, has very solid print quality (though it lags behind a few other options when it comes to full-color, photo-heavy books), and enough trim sizes to accomplish anything most authors and publishers will need to get done. Its close relationship with Amazon also makes getting a paperback version of your book up to complement the ebook version a walk in the park.

Basics:

- Start here: https://www.createspace.com
- The current ideal solution for most people publishing normal books, especially if you want to sell it online rather than in stores

Pros:

- Cheaper than most alternatives
- Easy to use, compared to alternatives
- Baked-in Amazon integration
- High-quality printing for most books

Cons:

- Lags a bit in quality when it comes to picture books
- No print runs or returns, which could be good to have in some circumstances
- Limited trim sizes, binding options, and finishes compared to Lightning Source

Lightning Source

Lightning Source is the once-king of the POD world, though now it's playing second-fiddle to Amazon's CreateSpace. This position doesn't mean it's any less useful than it once was, however, and in some areas in particular, it still handedly beats it's more popular rival.

As mentioned above, Lightning Source's big advantages are in distribution and print options. You can print hardcover books and a wider variety of trim sizes (larger, smaller, and more exotic shapes). It's also got you covered if you want to order a reasonably large batch of books, or if you want to allow returns for the bookstores who stock your work (which is standard practice for most traditional publishers).

That being said, part of why Lightning Source has floundered in the past several years is that it's more expensive than CreateSpace, and most people don't need the optimizations they offer. While Lightning Source offers more of the professional tools publishers and indie authors have traditionally needed in their arsenal, many of those tools are now irrelevant, and their potential clients are no longer seeing the benefits of, say, being able to offer matte covers when a glossy is almost as good, and the platforms offering glossy covers are so much easier to use, better connected with the sales channels they want to sell through, and cheaper all around.

Still, Lightning Source is a great option if you're looking to have truly professional work done and don't mind the slight administrative muddling and increased prices.

Basics:

- Start here: https://www1.lightningsource.com/default.aspx
- Former number one in the POD space, Lightning Source is now a very capable number two, with some pro-level advantages over the dominant CreateSpace

Pros:

- More trim options and binding options
- Better options for dealing with bookstores and other real-world distribution centers

Cons:

- More expensive
- A little more cumbersome to use than alternatives
- Less likely to be latently stocked by online platforms (like Amazon, which prefers their own POD platform, CreateSpace)

Lulu / Blurb

If CreateSpace and Lightning Source compete for dominance of the normal, written-word book space, Lulu and Blurb are doing the same for photo-heavy book dominion. Both work similarly, both produce high-quality products, and both have a slight stigma attached: that they are consumer-grade printers, not suitable for professionals.

But that stigma is unwarranted in both cases, because both companies have tools and end-products that justify their use in certain circumstances.

Lulu's strength is in its ease of use and low cost of entry. It's generally significantly cheaper than Blurb and has a thriving community as a result.

Blurb's strength is in its higher-quality printing (some would say highest in the color POD industry) and production software (which some consider to be a benefit, while others see it as a hurdle). It's community of users is smaller, but the work usually looks a bit better designed and printed.

The choice between these two options is largely a matter of taste, because the quality difference would not be noticed by most readers, and the ease-of-use for both options is pretty accessible. At the end of the day, it's not so much a Coke and Pepsi differentiation as a Coke and Diet Coke gap. We'll leave it to your judgement which is which.

Basics:

- Start here for Lulu: http://www.lulu.com/publish/books/
- Start here for Blurb: http://www.blurb.com
- Both provide high-quality POD color books at reasonable prices, especially compared to options available from CreateSpace and Lightning Source

Pros:

- Great quality images and binding
- Easy to use, even for luddites
- A lot of import options available between the two services, everything from automatic blog importing to photo album uploading

Cons:

- Often considered to be less professional than competing services because they focus on making everything so consumer-grade, rather than offering a lot of pro-level tools
- Neither plays as well with Amazon and other online bookstores as CreateSpace and Lightning Source— more ideal for printing and ordering hand-sell copies than selling on their respective online platforms
- You lose some degree of control with both, though

Blurb also includes their copyright information in your book, which may be off-putting to some

In-Person Sales Options

Square

A relative newcomer in the payment processing world, Square hit the scene with a bang a few years ago, and since then it has handedly taken over the mobile payment processing world with a simple offering: a credit card swiping device that plugs into your phone, tablet, or other mobile device.

It's a simple change, but a big enough deal to have changed the perspective of many smaller shops, restaurants, and indie authors overnight. Rather than being forced to purchase a massive card processing terminal and pay excessive usage costs, you plug a tiny device into the headphone jack of your iPhone, iPad, Android phone or tablet, and swipe. The Square app takes the card's information and allows you to enter all kinds of data about the sale (if you like), including the name and email of the customer, a photo of the item being sold, or random notes on the purchase. The receipt can then be emailed to the customer and info about the sale is saved to your account. Card not working? Forget the swiper dongle? No worries, you can enter the card information by hand.

You also have two payment options: either 2.75% of each swiped transaction, or 3.5% + 15¢ of each manually entered transaction. Both offerings are quite a bit cheaper than traditional credit card terminals.

Basics:

- Start here: https://squareup.com
- Sign up, wait for the free mobile dongle to arrive in the mail, download app, and start swiping. Pretty much the easiest way for an individual to process credit cards. Only cost is 2.75% of each wiped transaction or 3.5% + 15¢ of each manually entered transaction.

Pros:

- Incredibly simple to use
- Plugs in to device you probably already have with you, but there's also an iPad terminal available
- Get paid the next day—money from card swipes is deposited straight to your bank account

Cons:

- There aren't any real downsides to using this system

Paypal Here

Paypal, still a dominant force in the online payments world, saw what Square managed to do with mobile card processing and decided to provide their own version, called PayPal Here (PPH).

PayPal Here works essentially the same way as Square —plug in a device to your phone or tablet and swipe cards, and then complete the sale in the associated app. PPH does have a few advantages over Square, and also one major disadvantage. The advantages are that you get paid on the same day the card is processed (the money appears in your PayPal account, at least), and it takes .05% less from your transaction (2.7% instead of 2.75%). You can also accept PayPal payments in person (just enter the appropriate info into the app), checks, and invoices.

The big downside of using PayPal Here is also an advantage: it relies on PayPal to process everything. Your money goes into your PayPal account, and you can use the money right away using PayPal online, a PayPal debit card, or withdraw it into your bank account. The reason this might be a downside is that PayPal has a reputation for sometimes putting holds on accounts without explanation, hassling people for having strange activity on their account, and essentially being unresponsive when contacted by users who are trying to get access to their money. This is not common, but it happens often enough that many people avoid PayPal when possible and prefer to remove the intermediary step, funneling money directly into their bank account, rather than hitting the PayPal service first.

Basics:

- Start here: https://www.paypal.com/webapps/mpp/credit-card-reader
- Easy to use, free dongle to plug into your devices, costs 2.7% of every transaction

Pros:

- Makes good use of PayPal network to allow for more payment options

Cons:

- Makes use of PayPal network
- Dongle is kind of ugly compared to Square's

Cash

I probably don't have to sell you on this option, and there isn't a service available to enable it, but hand-selling and accepting only cash is a time-worn tradition among authors and small publishers, and it's especially effective when combined with one of the above credit card-processing options. Accepting credit cards allows more people to purchase books, and especially if you offer some kind of deal (buy two, get both at a discounted price), folks will be more likely to pick up a few books rather than just one.

That being said, cash is easier than swiping, and as a result it's smart to keep change on hand and sell your books for nice, round prices ($7, not $6.97, though $5 or $10 is even better). This is also a good opportunity to note that anyplace, anytime can be a sales channel, so long as you have books on hand and people who are willing to hear about your book. Get creative.

Basics:

- No set up necessary and easy to use, so long as you have change on hand

Pros:

- Most people have some kind of cash on hand
- Works perfectly in conjunction with a mobile payment processor

Cons:

- Not everyone has cash on hand, and not necessarily enough to buy a book or three
- It can be hard to keep enough change on hand, especially if you're on the road

Non-Standard Options

HTML / Blog

Not all sales channels need to sell products. In some cases, you can provide your work as more of a service, providing access to your work for those who wish to pay for it.

It's important to note that there's a reason you don't see a lot of membership-paid blogs and writer sites out there. Putting a paywall around your site limits the number of people who will read your work significantly, and even the smallest price tag will be enough friction to keep folks from coming back. That being said, there are options available if you have a project that you think would be well-suited to such a model, and website- or blog-based published work is also a great way to share your work, should you decide to give it away for free (either as promo for other work, or because you're more concerned with building an audience than selling right now).

One of the easier ways to set up a website or blog is using a content management system called Wordpress. Wordpress is free, and it can be completely hands off (you sign up and start writing) or self-hosted and built. There's more ease-of-use with the former, and more control with the latter, including the ability to install a membership site plugin, which will allow you to charge for access to your work.

Of course, if you're just looking to share a few pieces of

work, rather than an ongoing series of writings, an HTML website will do just fine. You can pick up a template at depositories like ThemeForest, or learn to build your own (a skill that will be very handy moving forward).

Basics:

- Start here for a free Wordpress setup: https://wordpress.com
- Start here if you want to self-host: https://wordpress.org
- Incredible variety of options, in terms of different blogging software and layouts for websites
- Costs anywhere from nothing to hundreds of dollars, depending on what you're trying to achieve

Pros:

- Can be super lightweight and easy to set up
- Lots and lots of options

Cons:

- Not ideal for selling—far better for giving stuff away (which can be part of the selling process)
- You need to know what you want before you start producing—there are few limitations

Issuu / Scribd

Document library sites like Issuu and Scribd are great ways to present your books to the world, making them available to share and page through with intuitive interfaces, so long as you have a PDF file to share and an audience to share it with.

The main advantage these sites offer over blogging or building a website for your work is that there is a community of people perusing the documents uploaded, which means you stand a chance of having your work discovered organically. The presentation of your work is also quite beautiful, and there are many options for sharing and embedding your work elsewhere from these sites, should you choose to.

Scribd gives you the option of selling your work through their store, while Issuu gives you the option of signing up for a Pro account, removing ads and recommendations from the reading interface, and giving you the ability to monetize your work. Both services do an okay job of this, though the real power of both (like with blogs and websites) is presenting your work in an elegant, easy-to-use format that allows and encourages sharing. To that end, these two services are top notch. For selling, they're just okay.

Basics:

- Start here for Issuu: http://issuu.com/publish
- Start here for Scribd: https://www.scribd.com/upload-document
- Elegant interfaces for sharing published work, with excellent sharing and embedding options
- Issuu Pro (which removes ads from the reading interface and allows you to put it on sale or take subscriptions) costs $19/month
- Scribd costs 20% of transaction price plus $.25 per sale.

Pros:

- Great platforms if you're looking to promote your work with free books, short stories, or the like
- Excellent sharing and embedding options, and a great reading experience across devices

Cons:

- Not ideal for selling your work
- Neither have huge audiences, so sharing from the site and pulling people back to your work is your best bet

Mailchimp / TinyLetter

Publishing doesn't always mean creating something static —it can also mean creating something and delivering it to the reader via email. Newsletter services help you accomplish this quite easily, and modern newsletter services allow you to serve your work up beautifully and reliably, and in many cases cheap or free.

There are many different paid newsletter services available, but the one with the best look and ease of use is handedly Mailchimp (there are some people who prefer Aweber, but in most cases they either appreciate the ample marketing tools, or promote it because of its generous affiliate program). When it comes to straight up usability and design, Mailchimp's drag-and-drop interface is second to none, and their Forever Free plan allows you to use their services without paying a dime up to 2,000 subscribers and 12,000 emails per month. Not too shabby!

TinyLetter works a bit like Mailchimp's free plan, though it's even simpler. Rather than dragging-and-dropping your interface and images around, you write an email using a simple text editor (or send an email to a unique email address), and the message you write is then delivered to your list (which is limited to 2,000 people). It's completely free, and there's no premium option, so it'll stay free and simple.

There are pros and cons to both, and certain projects will warrant more or less control, so choose carefully. It is worth mentioning that Mailchimp once allowed for paid subscriptions but has recently phased that option out (while other newsletter services that focused on paid subscriptions—like letter.ly—have stopped allowing new sign ups). This is likely a temporary change up in the industry until a better way to process very small transactions comes along, but for the time being, unfortunately, there aren't any cheap, reliable ways to charge for subscription paid newsletters, so these delivery options are best used for promotional and free work, or as a means of distributing shorter pieces to your audience between longer, paid works.

Basics:

- Start here for Mailchimp: http://mailchimp.com
- Start here for TinyLetter: http://tinyletter.com
- Lots of free options, though Mailchimp will start charging more and more as your list grows into the thousands ($10 to $240)

Pros:

- Many ways to send your work out to your readers, which allows you to easily compose and publish completely from your phone, if you want to
- Cheap or free, no strings attached

Cons:

- No built-in way to make money from your work, so best used as a promotional tool or for experimental work

Social Media

It's not common, but it's possible to publish your work through social media platforms. And if done correctly, this can be a very impactful way of sharing your work and having it passed around to reach a new audience.

Choosing the right social media platform for your project is key. Twitter, for example, limits you to 140 characters, so unless your work is easily broken apart into chunks that size, Facebook might be a better option, with its 63,206 character limit. Longer form work is also shared quite a bit more on Facebook, whereas Twitter is more ideal for sharing links to work hosted elsewhere (even on Facebook).

If you think creatively, you can even come up with ways to use photo services like Instragram and Pinterest as publishing platforms—a real win, since both sites are highly trafficked and full of people who share things they like constantly. Try converting your words into images, or overlaying an appropriate image with a poem you've written. You could also publish your work as the comment, while the photo helps it get passed around. The sky is the limit, and if your work contains visual media in addition to words, there are a lot of opportunities within the social media world to publish it in a non-traditional way.

All that being said, there's absolutely no reliable way to monetize the work you share on social media. This option is best left to promotional and experimental work. Stuff you can afford to give away, to give people a taste of your work (you can link to your paid work in some cases, though not on every network).

Basics:

- Start here for Facebook: https://www.facebook.com
- Start here for Twitter: https://www.twitter.com
- Start here for Instagram: https://instagram.com
- Start here for Pinterest: http://pinterest.com
- Start here for Google Plus: https://plus.google.com
- Lots of opportunities to get creative with your work, maybe even having something go viral if it's shareable enough
- You'll need to present your work very differently if you use these platforms, since each has different length limits and different types of media get more attention than others

Pros:

- Incredibly shareable if done right
- Free to use
- Built-in audience of millions of people

Cons:

- Very impermanent—expect to publish and have everyone forget you did so a few minutes later
- No way to monetize
- Limiting in how you present your work

Podcasts

Podcasts are radio shows for the modern listener, sitting at their computer and listening to their iPhones, rather than listening to the radio and Walkman. The type of content you can share in a podcast is equally new-age. Rather than just music and radio shows, the podcast format allows you to present work audibly that might otherwise just sit quietly on the page.

Podcasts, like blog posts, tend to do best when made available for free and when sharing is encouraged, but there are a few ways to monetize. You can embed them in blog posts or websites, for one, making use of the aforementioned membership plugins. You could also sell individual episodes or sell subscriptions (monthly, yearly, or a season or collection of work).

Some podcast hosting services like Libsyn offer premium subscription plans, paid either monthly or by taking a percentage of your subscription payments. You can also monetize your work with podcasts by integrating advertising—something that most hosts offer, each using slightly different models.

Basics:

- Start here: http://www.libsyn.com
- Great way to present work to people who don't read much, or who listen to a lot of radio or podcasts

Pros:

- Early costs are reasonable (usually around $10-20/month to get started)
- Reach a whole new audience
- Many expansion options, ranging from monetization opportunities to custom mobile apps

Cons:

- Could be a distraction from writing, since it requires a completely new set of equipment and skills
- Requires that you build an audience, as there isn't much opportunity to gain readers organically

Vimeo / YouTube

Like podcasting, video renditions of your work offer up some very interesting opportunities, so long as you're willing to put in the time to learn to do it right and don't mind translating your work into vocal or visual performances.

Both Vimeo and YouTube have a lot of offerings beyond the standard, consumer-grade video opportunities. Both offer ways for members to make money from their work (you'll need a Pro account to do this on Vimeo, and they'll take 10% of all revenue you make therein, while YouTube offers advertising partnerships), and both offer an array of sophisticated tools for optimizing and publishing your work.

YouTube has an advantage in terms of organic traffic—you'll have to work for it, but there's a chance you could get foot traffic from viewers watching other videos. Vimeo doesn't have that same asset, but it is considered to be a more professional platform, so if you have an existing audience, it might be the better choice (less clutter, no ads, cleaner design aesthetic).

It's free to start working on both, though a Pro account on Vimeo will cost you $200/year.

Basics:

- Start here for Vimeo: https://vimeo.com
- Start here for YouTube: http://youtube.com

- There are many options available, but both YouTube and Vimeo provide many opportunities to share your work, and monetize it in some way
- Vimeo costs $200/year to use their full range of Pro-level tools

Pros:

- People love video and love to share video content
- Opportunity to extrapolate on your work and present it in a different form
- Tools required are easily acquired

Cons:

- Takes practice to do really good video work
- May take time to find correct format for presenting your work in video form
- Costly to use Vimeo's services, and YouTube's are plastered with ads

Further listening: Podcast: Sales Channels (http://asymmetrical.co/?powerpress_pinw=1548-podcast)

CHAPTER 6: HOW TO SUCCESSFULLY PROMOTE YOUR BOOK TO AN AUDIENCE

Celebrate Good Times...Come On!

Congratulations. If you've followed the steps outlined in Chapters 1–5—if you've written and edited and designed a cover for and formatted and then published your own Book—well then you are now an Independently Published Author. Bravo!

Take a moment to think about what that means. Look around: how many people do you know who've published a Book? Five? Fewer than five? If you're like most people, there's a good chance you're the only person you know who has actually published a Book—fewer still have published a Book that has gone through the same rigorous quality control as your Book.

This is something you can be proud of. Your Book has

the ability to be an asset for the rest of your life. Nothing can take that from you—not a lost job or a family emergency or tough economic times. Your Book is *your* Book forever, an asset for life.

So now what are you going to do with that asset? That's a whole 'nother story.

Well, ideally you'll sell it to people who are interested in reading it. Duh! But how do you find those people? How do you connect with an audience? How do you let the world know about your creation? How do you successfully promote your Book?

Before we chat about growing an audience, let's talk about the misconceptions we seem to have regarding this thing called *Going Viral*. Basically, we want you to strive for something else...

Skip the Virus, ahem, the Viral

Everyone wants it—the overnight success, the secret formula, the magic pill. The path of least resistance is endemic in our current culture. We all want to *Go Viral*.

But have we at any point stopped the pursuit of *Viral* for a moment and asked ourselves why? Is there a reason we try to create the viral video, the over-shared blog post, the retweeted tweet? Or are we all just Pavlov's dogs, drooling on command for a morsel of attention?

Maybe we're allergic to the magic pill, but our own

overnight success didn't happen, *ahem*, overnight. As far as we can tell, we've never had anything *Go Viral*. Viral content itself is but a well-crafted soundbite, which is, by definition, devoid of substance; soundbites have immediate appeal, but they lack staying power.

Going Viral will undoubtedly send a shedload of people your way—clicks and views and tweets. But is it the kind of traffic you want? Are they an engaged audience? Are they going to stick around? Or is *Going Viral* more like throwing a party with an open bar? Of course people will make an appearance, but what will keep them there when the free booze has dried up?

There is, however, an alternative. Instead of *Going Viral*, at Asymmetrical we focus on one thing: *Adding Value*. Habitually, before every tweet, every blog post, every Book we write, we ask ourselves, *Are we Adding Value? Are we contributing in a meaningful way?*

Adding Value is the only way to gain long-term buy-in, and it's one of the few ways to build trust. When people trust you, they are eager to share your message with the people they love. Contribution is a basic human instinct; we are intrinsically wired to share value with others. Viral or no, *trust* is the best way to spread your message. Without it, the exit is just a click away.

Paths to Reach Your Audience by Building a Platform

There are at least five paths to build an Audience by Adding Value:

1. **Blogging**. Blogging is one of the best (if not *the* best) ways to build an audience. We wouldn't be here preaching from the soapbox today if it wasn't for *Exile Lifestyle* and *The Minimalists*. That's because blogging allows you to own and control your own work, to direct people to your creations, and to share your ruminations with folks all over the world.

Must-read articles: How to Start a Successful Blog Today (http://www.theminimalists.com/blog) and Who the Hell Reads Your Blog Anyway? (http://www.theminimalists.com/blogging)

2. **Social Media**. Social media can be intimidating. You've got Facebook and Twitter and Google+ and Pinterest and Instagram and Tumblr and Vine and YouTube and Flickr and Goodreads, and those are just the platforms we use. (There are others that we've never tried out like, say, Path, Snapchat, Bebo, et al., but that doesn't mean that you have to ignore them.) Figuring out which platform(s) work best for *you* is the ticket. For us, Twitter works best; it is the social network we find the most value in, and thus it is the network we use most frequently.

We understand, however, that different people find value in different networks (for different reasons). If you're a photographer, then likely Flickr or Instagram will work best; if you're writing Young Adult Fiction, then Tumblr might be ideal because of its large share of teens; if you're connecting with bloggers and techies and the like, then maybe your time is best spent on G+; if recipes or products where images reign supreme are your thing, then Pinterest is worth a shot; if videos are your forte then Vine or YouTube is your jam; and if your audience is more traditional, then maybe a Facebook Fan Page is right up your alley.

The reason Twitter works best for us, though, is 3-fold: 1) Twitter allows us to Add Value to other people in a succinct way via a) short quotable (tweetable!) ruminations, b) sharing interesting things we're currently reading, watching, or listening to, and c) occasionally, but not too often, sharing our own links (N.B. a good rule of thumb here is that for every one (c) shared, you should share at least nine (a)'s and/or (b)'s; the fatal flaw we've noticed is always the folks who just do (c) with very little, if any, (a) or (b), which is an unforgivable sin and is tantamount to public masturbation (*v.s.* Going Viral); 2) because Twitter limits you to 140 characters, brevity is key, and 3) we use Twitter as a sort of curation system; our Twitter feeds are full of news and interesting people. We follow only people whose words/links/tweets add value to our lives. And because that changes from time to time, our Twitter streams are ever-changing. Facebook is great for connecting with people you went to highschool with, while Twitter is great for connecting with people you *wish* you went to highschool with.

Our advice if you're not already regularly using social media: Start today. Like right now. Seriously. Pick *one* platform and get good at it. Eventually, you can add other platforms, but don't take on too much at once. Get good at one thing before moving on. Discover what Adds Value and do that.

Our advice if you are already using social media but want to use it more effectively: Basically, see above. The advice isn't really different. Focus on getting good at one platform; freeze the others in the meantime and focus on only one for now.

Additional reading: Feel Free to Unsubscribe, Unfollow (http://www.theminimalists.com/follow)

Additional viewing: Joshua Becker's How to Use Twitter to Grow Your Platform (https://www.youtube.com/watch?v=NIbQn-7XkHc&feature=autoshare)

Additional perspective: Simplify Internet (http://zenhabits.net/unline).

3. **Events**. We all have the ability to sit on our side of the screen and network via blogs and social media, which is great, but we all also live in the real world, and in the real world business still happens face to face. You can connect with someone on, say, Twitter, but the real lasting connections tend to come from face-to-face interaction.

Hence, once you've connected on the Internet, it's important to find ways to connect in person, which means attending conferences you might not want to attend (SXSW, BEA, WDS, Blog World, etc.), joining groups or clubs, and going out of your way to spend time with people who share similar values and beliefs.

4. **Exchanging Value**. Pay it forward. When you Add Value to other people's lives it's important to do so without a specific agenda. Remember, it's not a *direct* exchange; it's not *quid pro quo*. From some people you will gain more value than you'll ever be able to repay (be thankful); likewise, you should seek to Add Value to as many lives as possible (be generous), expecting nothing in return. The nice thing about this is that it always works out in your favor—the more you give, the more you get. Call it karma or destiny or cause and effect, or call it whatever you want; whatever you call it, it works.

Additional reading: Paying It Way Forward (http:// exilelifestyle.com/paying)

5. **Be Shareworthy**. Whatever you do, whatever platforms or vehicles or avenues or other silly metaphors you use to reach an audience, make sure that you create things that are Shareworthy. We don't know about you, but when something Adds Value to our lives, the first thing we do is share it with people we care about. Ergo, if you Add Value, your message will spread.

These five paths, if done correctly, will allow you to

build an audience over time. Sure it will take time, but doesn't everything worth having take time?

As you build your audience, though, you'd be remiss if you didn't also attempt to promote your Book at the same time. Let's look at 10 tactics to help your Book reach new people...

Tactics to Help Your Book Reach New People

1. **Loss Leaders**. If you have more than one Book, this is a great strategy. That is, price one book low (say $1) as an introduction to your body of work. If the person who spends a buck on your Book loves it, then his or her propensity to purchase another (higher-priced) Book increases significantly. This happens with our Books all the time. Someone discovers our work via one of our blogs and then takes a chance on one of our lower-priced Books. If they love it, they often buy several more titles from our body of work. A word of warning: even though your loss-leader Book is inexpensive, it still has to be great; otherwise why would they pick up another one of your titles.

2. **Pricing**. Similar to #1 above, you can play around with pricing to see what works best for you. It's important to not undervalue your work while, at the same time, being cognizant of your marketplace. No sane person charges $37

for an eBook these days. So do your research; find out how much similar Books are selling for and then price yours accordingly. Remember, you can always adjust, up or down, accordingly.

Related reading: Death of the Marketing Penny (http:// asymmetrical.co/penny)

3. **Free**. There are two reasons why we sometimes make one of our Books free: 1) as an extreme version of loss-leading, and 2) when we're looking for another way for our work to spread (i.e., sometimes you create something you're so passionate about, something you're so happy with, something you believe will add so much value to other people's lives, that you feel compelled to give it away for free—you simply want to get it in as many hands as possible because you know it will Add Value). Either way, making your Book free breaks down the cost barrier, which is often the biggest hurdle for consumers. You have to be careful, though, because pricing your book at $0 can devalue its worth in some people's minds, and of course the money you'll earn from every free Book sold is $0 (unless of course your loss-leader strategy directs people to purchase your other Books).

Related Reading: What Is the Real Price of Free? (http:// inoveryourhead.net/what-is-the-real-price-of-free)

4. **Reviews**. You want readers to review your Book once they've read it. This is especially helpful on sites like Amazon and Goodreads, for two reasons: 1) it allows

readers to congregate around your work in a meaningful way, showing appreciation for Books in which they find value, and 2) the more reviews you get, the more it helps you get noticed (by readers who read reviews and by Amazon et al.'s algorithm). Hence, it's OK to ask readers (via your blog or social media) to leave a review. Just make sure you ask nicely. And don't be pushy. And don't ask too often; once will do. Also, no logrolling: don't ask people to leave a five star review; ask them to leave an honest review.

5. **Blog Reviews and Guest Posts**. At Asymmetrical we have a list of blogs with whom we regularly communicate. Often, those blogs are willing to review or share our books with their audience. Likewise, you should make your own list of blogs and websites with similar values and audiences (audiences you hope to reach). Ask them if they'd be willing to review your book on their blog (or do a guest post if that makes more sense). Remember, though, make sure you Add Value first. You shouldn't just email someone and say "Hey, do this for me!" without first finding ways to Add Value to their lives. That'd be tacky.

6. **Local Media**. Your local print, radio, and television outlets (as well as local blogs) love to feature feel-good pieces about local authors. Your new book is a great opportunity to get scads of local press coverage. Whenever we publish a new book, we reach out to all the editors and produces at the local newspaper, the local alternative presses, the local radio stations, and a few local news networks in an effort to create

local buzz around our new release. When done correctly, these efforts pay off immensely. When contacting these outlets, keep it short with just the most pertinent information: author bio, book synopsis, book cover. Make it known that you're local, too. That's important. Furthermore, it's easier to approach media outlets if you have a special event—e.g., a book signing—scheduled at a local bookstore (such an event adds legitimacy and gives the media a reason to cover your story).

7. **Tour**. Touring is a fun way to meet readers, but you don't have to have a huge audience to conduct a book tour. And you don't have to tour all over the country either. Hell, your tour can consist of one or two stores if you'd like. Again, events like this will give the local media reasons to feature you and your work. They also create a sense of urgency.[27]

8. **Speaking**. Are there nearby events that pertain to your book at which you can speak? Universities, libraries, and clubs welcome authors with open arms as long as your Book's topic is congruent with theirs.

9. **Indie Bookstores**. Besides the local media, guess who else loves local authors: local Indie Bookstores. Before you become a local celebrity via the local media scene, make sure you've connected with all the Indie Bookstores in your city, as well as nearby cities. Fostering these relationships will go a long way.

10. **Hand-Selling**. Hand-selling is a catch-all term for DIY selling. We at Asymmetrical often call it out-of-the-trunk selling. Anytime we have any type of event—a speaking gig, a conference, a tour, a group we meet with—we make sure we have a box of Books with us ready to sell. That way, when people ask you about your Book, which they will, you'll be ready. Oh, and good news: You don't have to take only cash either. Square allows you to swipe credit cards via your smartphone or tablet.

Further listening: Podcast: Successfully Promote Your Book (http://asymmetrical.co/?powerpress_pinw=1569-podcast)

HELLO, INDIE AUTHOR

You've done it. You've written a book, published it, and learned how to successfully share your work with others. You've done something most people never do.

So now what do you do?

When we at Asymmetrical finish the publishing process, when we finish writing and editing and formatting and distributing and sharing our work, there's only one thing we *can* do: All of it. Again. From the beginning.

We're Independent Authors. And now, so are you.

If you have any questions, thoughts, or comments, drop us a line at howdy@asymmetrical.co. We love hearing from you.

RESOURCES

Ultimately, we know that you can successfully publish your Book entirely on your own—we have the empirical first-hand experience to prove it—but if you want assistance in certain areas, then the Asymmetrical team is here to help.

Visit the Asymmetrical Studio to find a slew of professional services, resources, and classes you might find useful on your publishing journey: http://asymmetrical.co/services

ABOUT ASYMMETRICAL PRESS

Asymmetrical Press is a publishing house based in Missoula, Montana, run by indie authors, for indie authors—publishing for the indie at heart.

ENDNOTES AND REFERENCES

1. "JFM's How to Write Better Class" *The Minimalists* — http://www.theminimalists.com/class/

2. "Don't Flinch: A Conversation with Julien Smith" *The Minimalists* http://www.theminimalists.com/flinch/

3. *The Flute Player*, by Shawn Mihalik — http://asymmetrical.co/the-flute-player

4. "Brooklyn-based Lit Mag's Twitter Experiment" *The Brooklyn Ink* — http://thebrooklynink.com/2009/11/30/5809-brooklyn-based-lit-mags-twitter-experiment/

5. Asymmetrical Community Forums — http://asymmetrical.co/community/

6. "First Thing in the Morning: Why I Wake at 3:30 AM" *The Minimalists* — http://www.theminimalists.com/morning/

7. *As a Decade Fades*, by Joshua Fields Millburn — http://www.theminimalists.com/aadf/

8. U.S. Copyright Office forms — http://www.copyright.gov/forms/

9. "Where have all the editors gone, and why are publishers making you pay for editing?" *Venture Galleries* — http://venturegalleries.com/featured-vg-blog/where-have-all-the-editors-gone-and-why-are-publishers-making-you-pay-for-editing/

10. Createspace Custom Cover Services — https://www.createspace.com/

Services/CustomCover.jsp

11. Createspace Online Cover Creator — https://www.createspace.com/Tools/CoverCreator.jsp

12. Book Cover Design, *99 Designs* — http://99designs.com/book-cover-design

13. Photoshop Star — http://www.photoshopstar.com

14. Lynda.com — http://www.lynda.com

15. "Intro to Design for Publishing" *Exile Lifestyle* — http://exilelifestyle.com/intro-to-design-for-publishing/

16. "How to Create a Cover PDF for Your Book" *Createspace* — https://www.createspace.com/Products/Book/CoverPDF.jsp

17. "Kerning" *Wikipedia* — http://en.wikipedia.org/wiki/Kerning

18. "Half title" *Wikipedia* — http://en.wikipedia.org/wiki/Half_title

19. "A Beginner's Guide to Using Scrivener" — http://asymmetrical.co/community/threads/a-beginners-guide-to-using-scrivener.173/

20. Bowker.com — http://www.bowker.com/en-US/products/servident_isbn.shtml

21. KindleGen http://www.amazon.com/gp/feature.html/ref=amb_link_3576280 42_1?ie=UTF8&docId=1000765211&pf_rd_m=ATVPDKIKX0DER&pf_rd_s=center-6&pf_rd_r=1TMY9QP21ZFEE6WPAJG5&pf_rd_t=1401&pf_rd_p=1343256962&pf_rd_i=1000729511

22. KDP Select — https://kdp.amazon.com/select

23. Amazon Payments — https://payments.amazon.com

24. iBooks Author — http://www.apple.com/ibooks-author/

25. iTunes University — http://www.apple.com/education/ipad/itunes-u/

26. "Squarespace Commerce is Here" *Squarespace Blog* — http://blog.squarespace.com/blog/squarespace-commerce-is-here/

27. Check out our special tour podcast here, where we elaborate on our own touring experiences: http://asymmetrical.co/asymmetrical-podcast-episode-1/http://asymmetrical.co/asymmetrical-podcast-episode-1/

Printed in Great Britain
by Amazon

23838680R00088